TOM MARIONI

SCULPTURE
and
INSTALLATIONS
1969-1997

ISBN 1-891300-09-1

Thanks to the da Vinci Society
for its generous support in the production of this catalog.

Tom Marioni is represented by the Gallery Paule Anglim, San Francisco;
Crown Point Press, San Francisco; and the Margarete Roeder Gallery, New York City.

SOUND SCULPTURE

FREE **BEER**

DRUM BRUSHING

MOCA **WEDNESDAY**

YELLOW LIGHT

SHADOW **DRAWING**

FEATHER WRITING

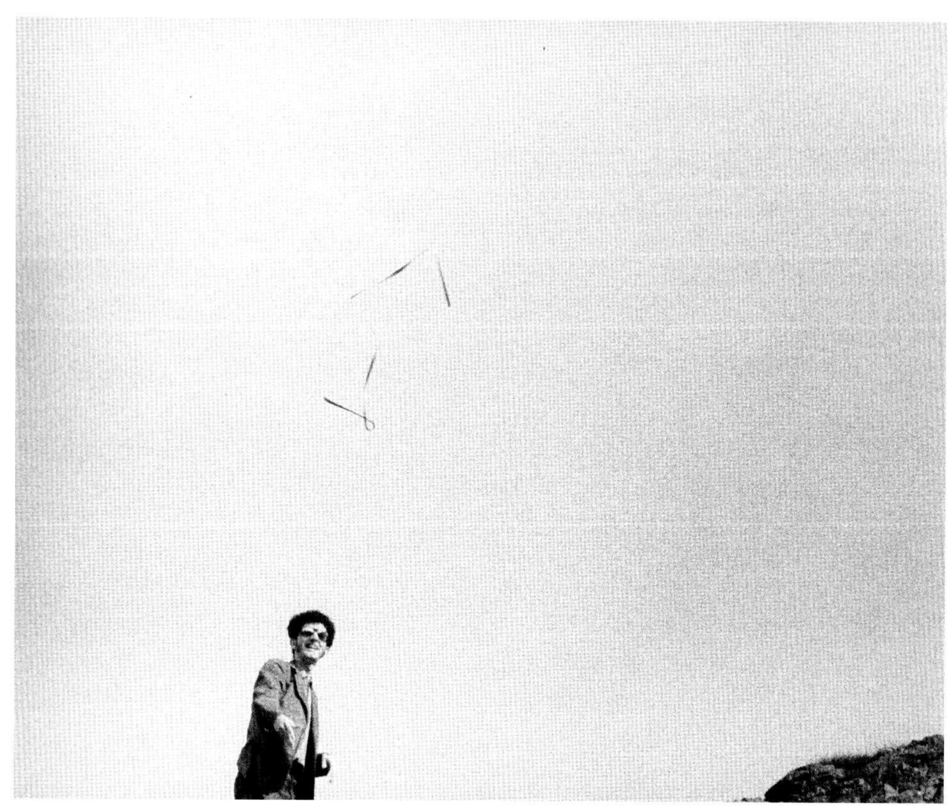

One Second Sculpture, 1969. Action. San Francisco. Instrument made from a metal tape measure that flies open like a spring in one second, making a loud sound. The object leaves the hand as a circle, makes a drawing in space and falls to the ground as a line.

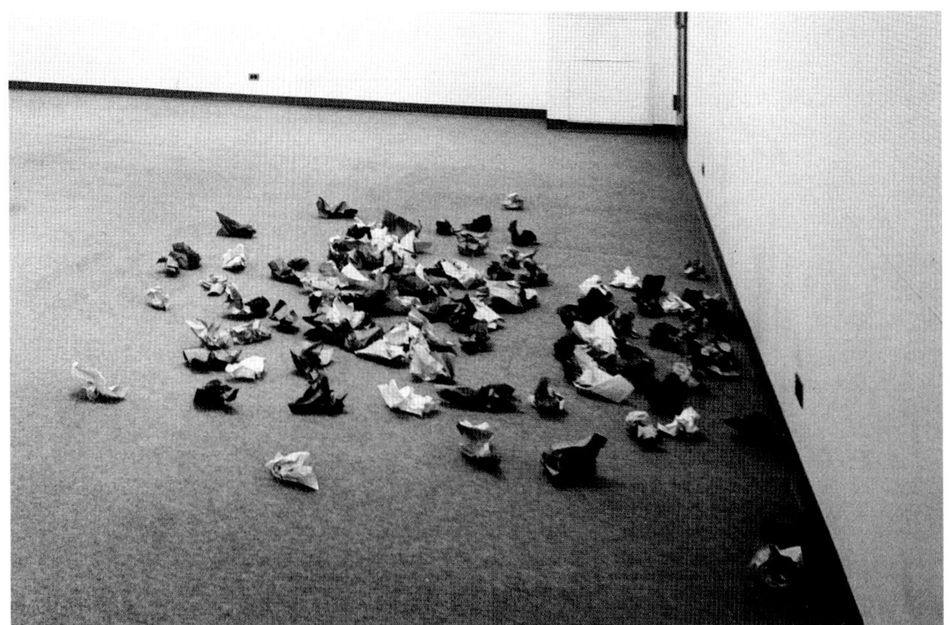

Birds in Flight, 1969. Installation for the exhibition, *The Return of Abstract Expressionism,* Richmond Art Center, California.

I was curator of the Richmond Art Center where this group exhibition was held. I included this work under the name Allan Fish and mailed in the following instructions for the curator to use in installing the work. After this, I used the name Allan Fish for all my work until 1971 when I no longer was a curator.

Instructions sent:

Enclosed is a packet of multi-colored construction paper. To install sculpture, sit in a chair about ten feet from a wall. Take one sheet at a time and crumple each one, as if you were in a hurry and throwing it into a wastepaper basket. Throw each piece at the wall, trying to keep them generally in a confined area. The result should be multi-colored birds at the moment of flight after being frightened by the stamping of feet.

History of Wednesdays

Free Beer, 1973-4. Free beer every Wednesday afternoon in the Museum of Conceptual Art (MOCA) while artists' video tapes were shown.

Wednesdays, 1976-present. A weekly open house.

Cafe Society, 1976-84, in Breen's Cafe, downstairs from MOCA, every Wednesday from 2-4 p. m. In 1979, Breen's closed and Wednesdays moved next door to Jerry and Johnny's bar. In 1981-2, artist's credit cards good for free beer on meeting days were issued to all artists on request. This was aided by a grant to MOCA by the NEA.

Academy of MOCA, 1984-90. MOCA closed but Wednesday meetings continued 4-6 p. m. In 1989 on October 17, 5:04 p.m., an earthquake closed Jerry and Johnny's permanently. Temporary Wednesdays continued at first in the House of Shields bar and later at the Capp Street Project.

Archives of MOCA, 1990-92, in my studio at 22 Hawthorne Street. People started leaving their own bottles for future visits. House rules were established. In 1992 the archives went to the University of California Art Museum in Berkeley and the name Archives of MOCA was dropped.

Cafe Wednesday, 1992-present, in my studio at the front of the same building. My former studio is now the bar of Hawthorne Lane Restaurant.

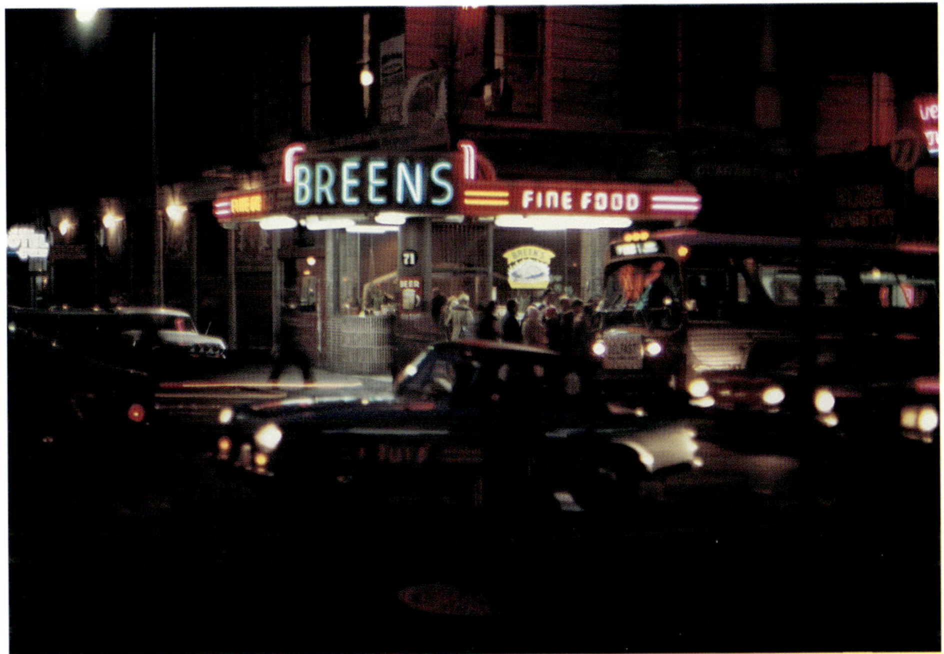

MOCA, Museum of Conceptual Art, founded in 1970 by Tom Marioni, closed in 1984. A space for performance/actions and installation sculpture. Located at 75 Third Street, San Francisco above Breen's Bar and Restaurant which functioned as a reception center and artists' saloon.

An Artist's Right to Remain Silent

San Francisco Chronicle Sept. 29, 1977, Thomas Albright.

For some years now, Tom Marioni's Museum of Conceptual Art has followed an extraordinary — and perhaps prophetic — policy of presenting exhibitions only when Marioni came across work that he felt imperative to exhibit.

In contrast with the potpourri of fillips with which most museums occupy much of their schedules and seek to justify their institutional existences during the long intervals between activities of genuine value, the Museum of Conceptual Art has as its sole continuing "program" a weekly open house for artists at Breen's saloon downstairs from its quarters on third street.

From all reports, the usual tenor of conversation — revolving around events within the singular international circles wherein conceptualists' reputations are made and broken — and the volume of brew imbibed, effectively belie any resemblance to the early Christian catacombs. Yet the analogy to a community of religious dropouts is too provocative entirely to pass by, and the principle involved too crucial to overlook: the right and obligation of artist — of all of us, but especially artists — to remain silent, except when there is something to say.

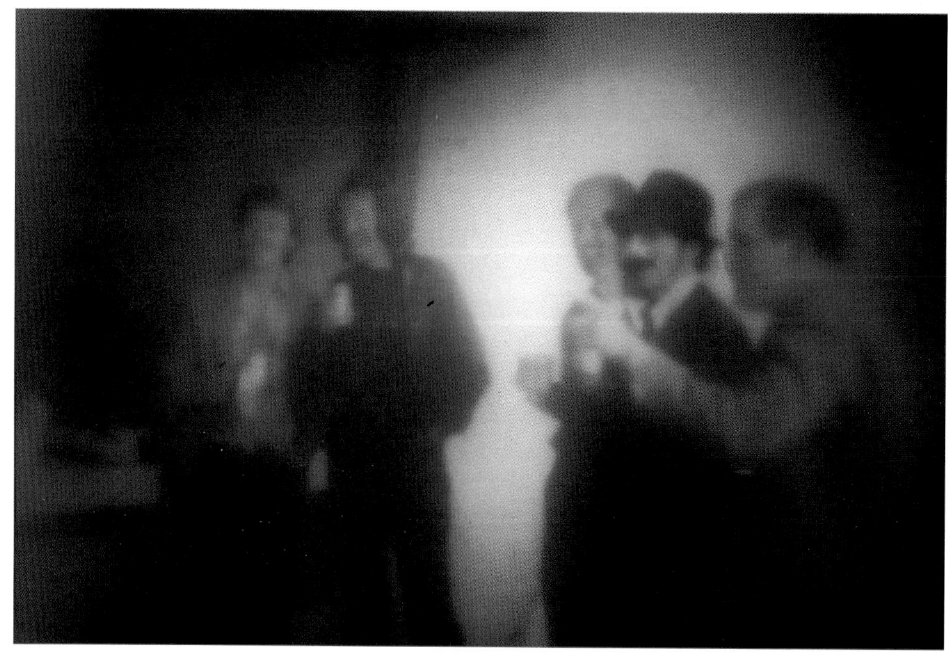

The Act of Drinking Beer with Friends is the Highest Form of Art. 1970. Event and exhibition (the debris was exhibited). Oakland Art Museum, California.

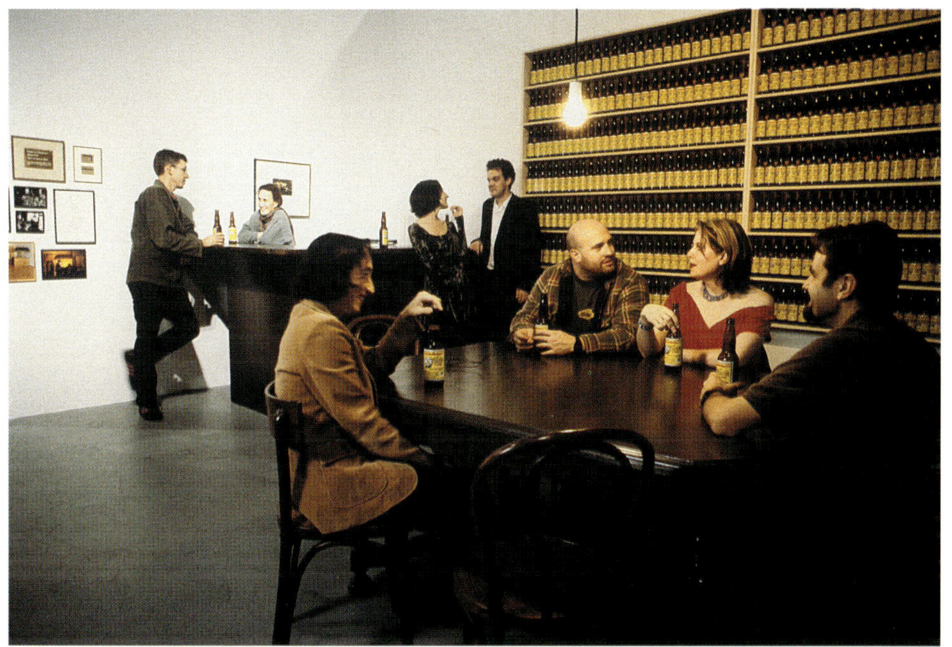

The Act of Drinking Beer with Friends is the Highest Form of Art. 1970, (Cafe Wednesday) recreated 1995 for *Reconsidering the Object of Art 1965-1975* at the Los Angeles Museum of Contemporary Art. Installation with free beer. Los Angeles.

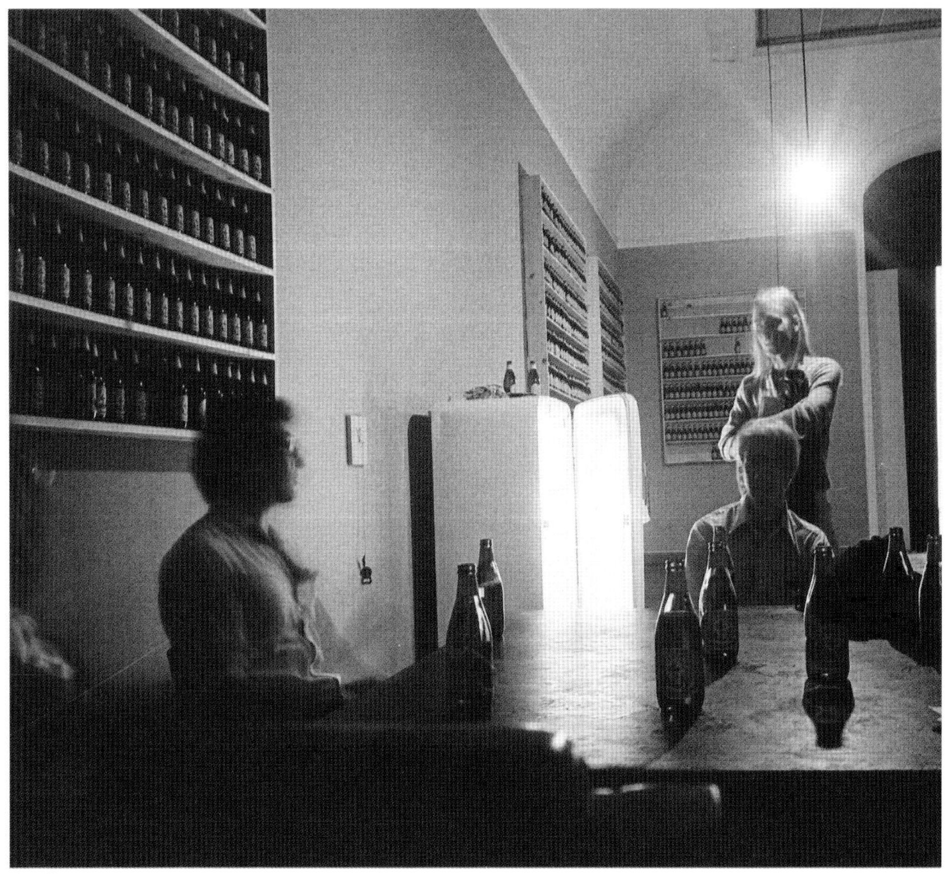

The Museum of Conceptual Art at the San Francisco Museum of Modern Art. 1979
Installation with free beer, San Francisco.

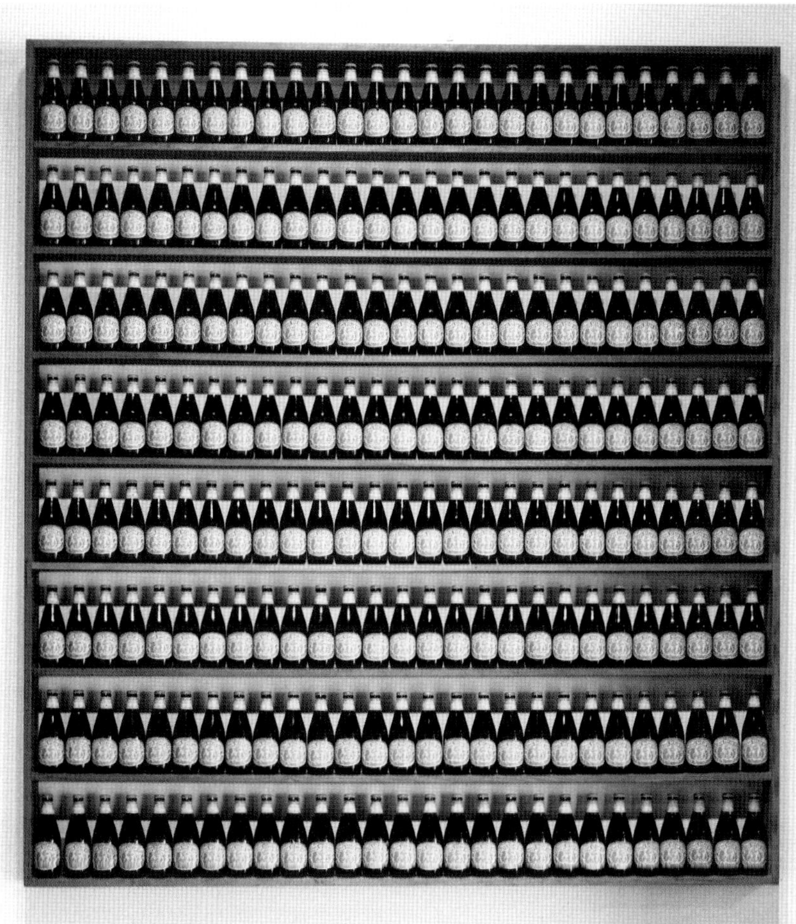

An Aid to Communication, 1979. Wood shelves and Anchor Steam beer bottles. 6'×6'×5". Collection Newport Harbor Art Museum, Newport Beach, California.

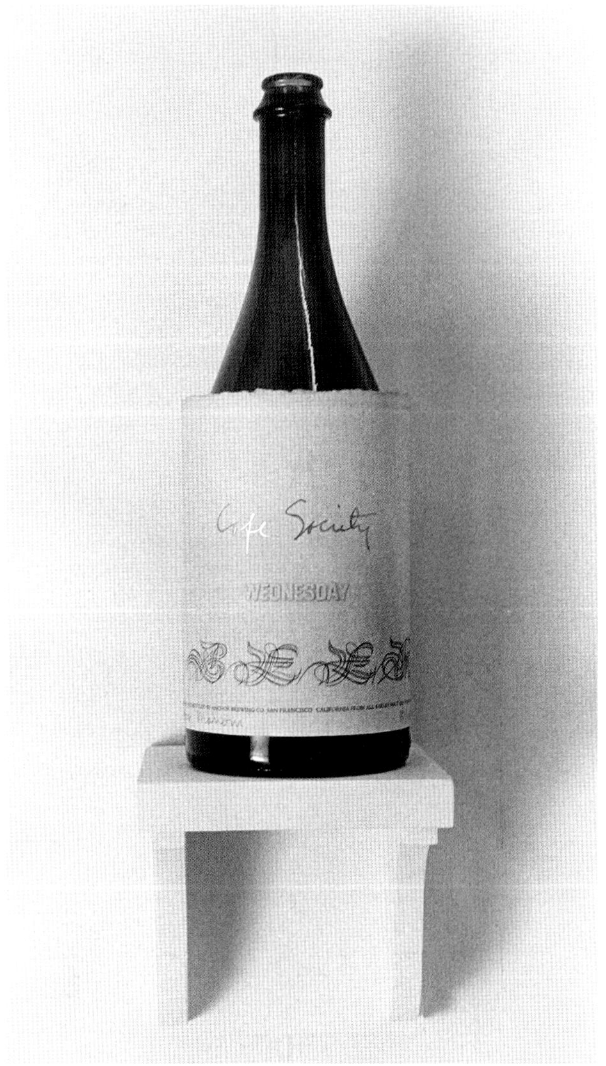

Cafe Society Beer, Edition 100, 1979. Soft ground etching mounted on a champagne bottle filled with beer. Bottled by the Anchor Steam Beer Company. Published by Crown Point Press, San Francisco. Instructions included with each bottle: This is a social work of art. To complete the artwork, the beer must be consumed, shared by at least two people.

1979 Manifesto

I've realized that my concept of performance art is old fashioned. It's old fashioned to insist that performance art is sculpture evolved into the fourth dimension. Something I learned from Miles Davis was that by turning his back on the audience when he played, he was an artist working. He said once that he was a musician not a performer. I have held onto my notion of the sculpture action where the action is directed at the material I'm manipulating instead of at the audience, like in theater. I can see this is a 60's European idea of this kind of art. In '70 when I started MOCA as a specialized sculpture action museum, I made my own rules and defined conceptual art as idea-oriented situations not directed at the production of static objects. Now the break from the object isn't an issue anymore. Ten years ago it was important to make a statement against materialism by making actions instead of objects. Now with some artists in my generation there's a return to the object, not as an end in itself, but as material to explain a function, like before the Renaissance where the object was used in a social, architectural or religious way. But the 70's is, and the 80's probably will be, a cosmetic age of decoration and theatricality.

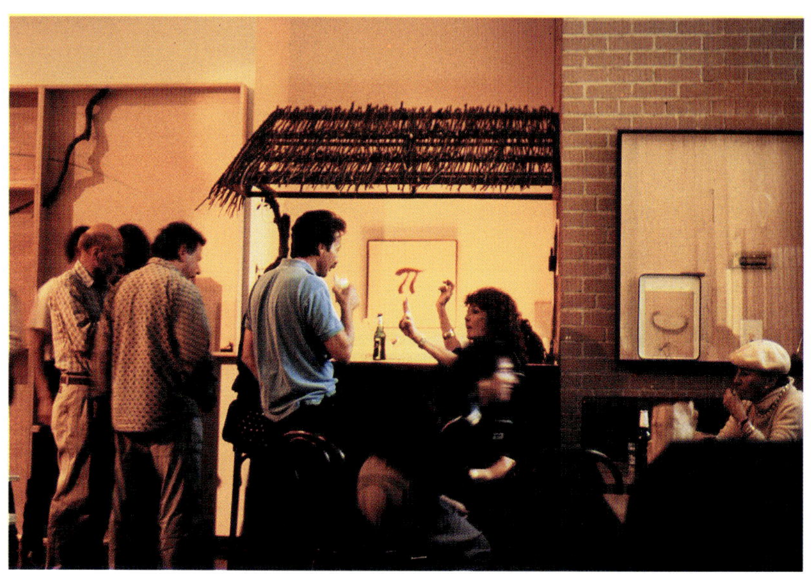

Studio with **Cafe Wednesday** in progress, 1992. San Francisco.

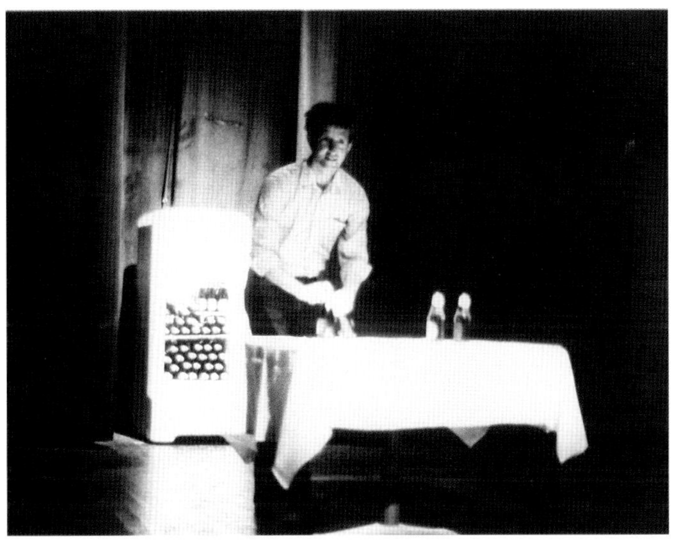

A Social Action, 1982. Action. Intersection Theater, San Francisco.

Marioni: A Master Illusionist's Act

San Francisco Chronicle Aug. 17, 1982, Thomas Albright.

…Marioni appears on an almost empty stage, carrying a funky portable record player, which he places on a small table near one wall, and a briefcase, from which he removes a white tablecloth, spreading it over a larger table at stage center. He pulls aside a curtain to expose a refrigerator filled to the brim with beer.

He opens a beer, takes a 35 mm camera from his briefcase, attaches its lens, loads it, takes out a tripod, puts it together and mounts the camera on it. He extracts a record, takes it to the record player, removes its lid, which he nails to a wall; puts the record on.

As the sound comes up — easy listing air-flo jazz — Marioni sits behind the big table, attaching a sheet of sandpaper to his fingers with masking tape. He walks to the far wall and proceeds to sand a small area of it.

Eventually, Marioni finishes the sanding, removes the sandpaper from his hand, returns to the wall, buffs it, sits again behind the table, and fiddles with some other objects taken from the briefcase. These turn out to be sticks of yellow chalk. With them, he begins to write: C A E — no, the E loses its bottom leg to become an F. Another F follows: C A F F. but the second F at the last minute gains a line to become an E: C A F E.

Marioni goes back over each letter, several times making them thicker and thicker. When the "sign" is done, he moves to his camera and takes its picture.

All this occurs at a measured, unhurried, but not draggy pace, the tempo of a solitary person going about routine activity, unconcerned, but not unaware that an audience is present. It maintains a lightness of touch which, for performance art, verges on the preciousness of French film comedy, together with a sustained undercurrent of anticipation, if not exactly suspense.

And then, as he hangs a little framed picture, (the sandpaper) on the wall near the yellow CAFE sign, you suddenly become aware that something dramatic has happened: Using the sparest symbolic shorthand, and directly before your eyes, Marioni has completely transformed the psychological dimensions of the space in which he has been performing from a neutral tabula rasa to an intimately personal space where an artist quietly works, and thence into a more public, or "social" area with the feeling of — well, of a new North Beach cafe just ready to open its doors for business.

And at just this point, the piece ends with Marioni asking the audience to join him on stage for beer. Or almost ends.

After everyone has moved to the front of the theater to be served a bottle from the refrigerator, Marioni gives the dimensions of reality a final twist, moving, with his tripod and camera, back into the rows of seats, where he starts taking pictures of the audience, which has now become the performers.

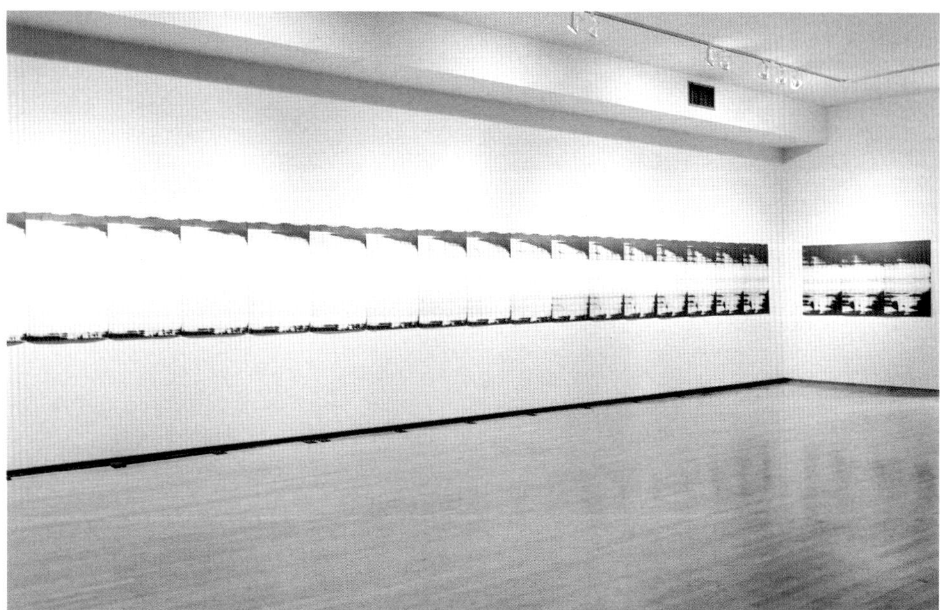

Process Print, 1970. 225 sheets of paper were run through an offset printing press with no image on the plate. The paper gradually picked up the ink until it was solid brown. Exhibited as an entire edition. DeSaisset Art Museum, University of Santa Clara, California.

The Creation, a Seven Day Performance, 1972. I lived in the gallery for a week making art actions each day that related to the creation of the world as described in the Bible. Reese Palley Gallery, San Francisco.

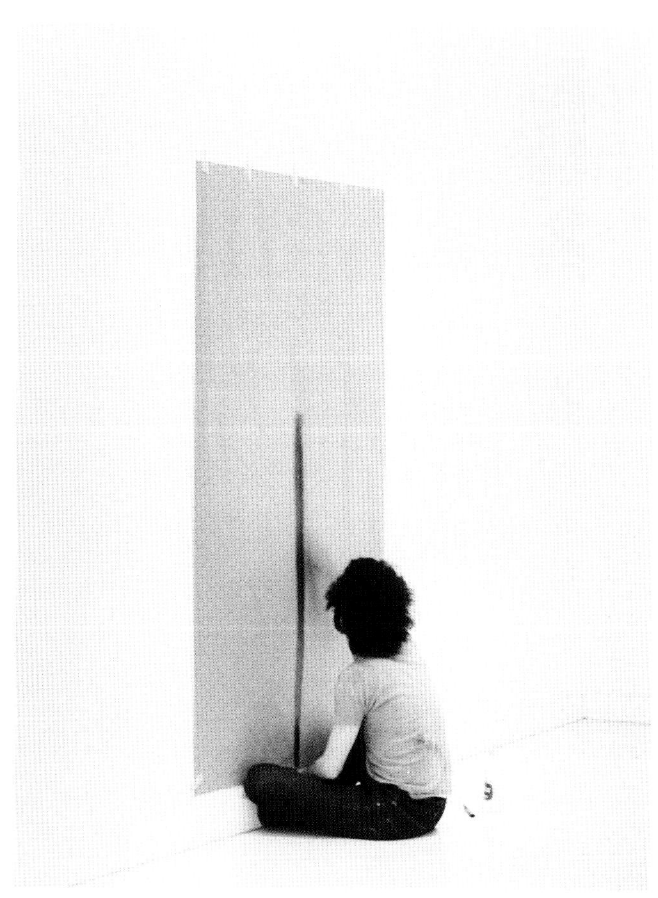

Tree, Drawing a Line as Far as I Can Reach, 1972 from
The Creation, a Seven Day Performance. Drawing, pencil on
paper, collection Oakland Museum, California.

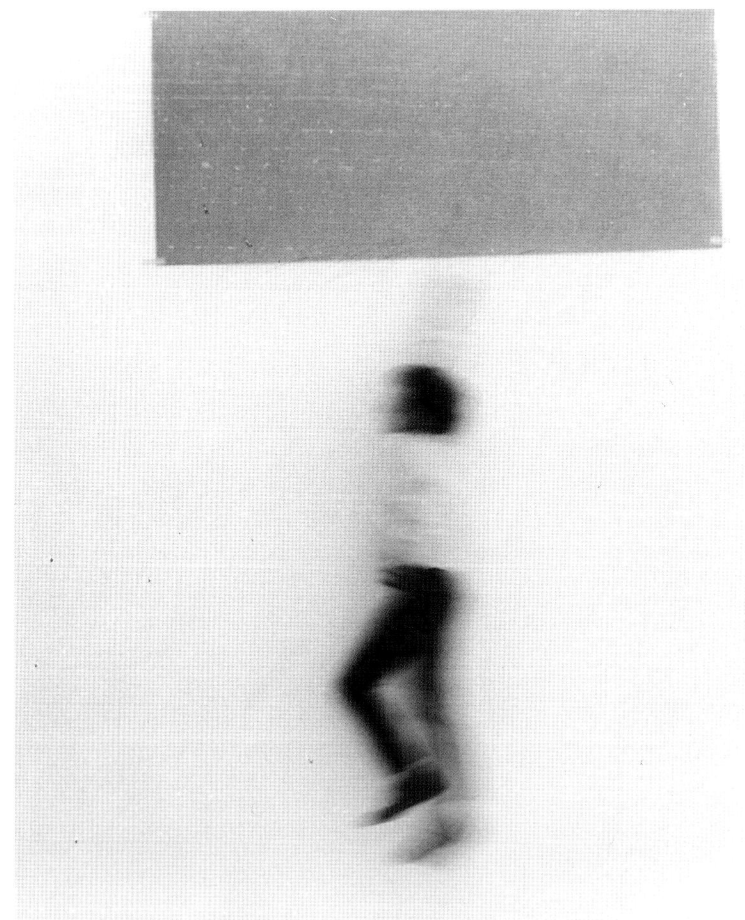

Bird, Running and Jumping with a Pencil, Marking the Paper while Trying to Fly, 1972 from *The Creation, a Seven Day Performance.* Pencil on paper.

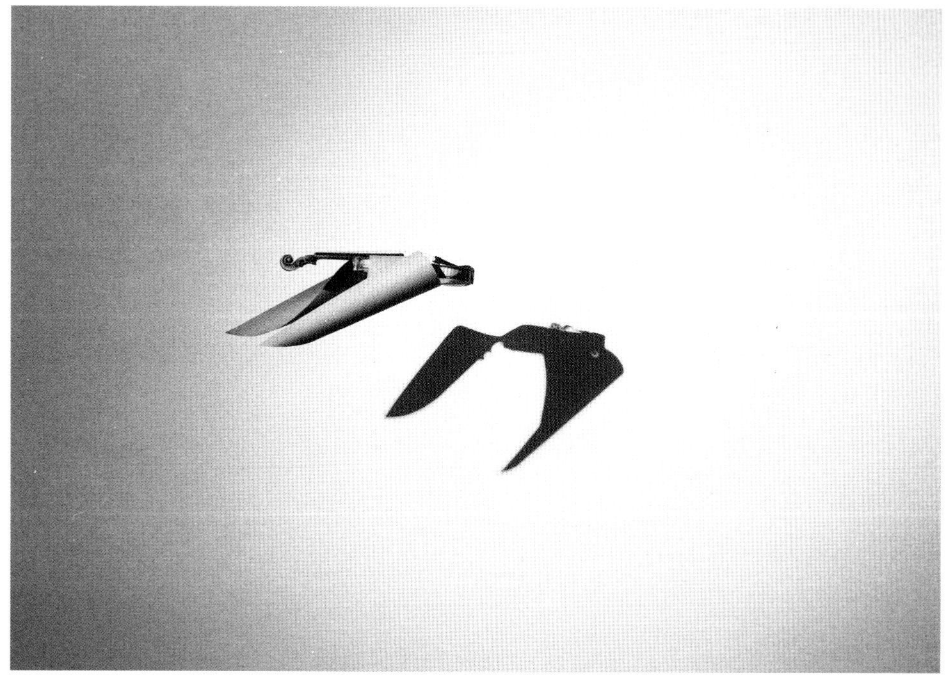

Violin Bird, 1972. Sculpture with shadow. 8×8×3'. Used in a performance/action, Richard Demarco Gallery, Edinburgh, Scotland.

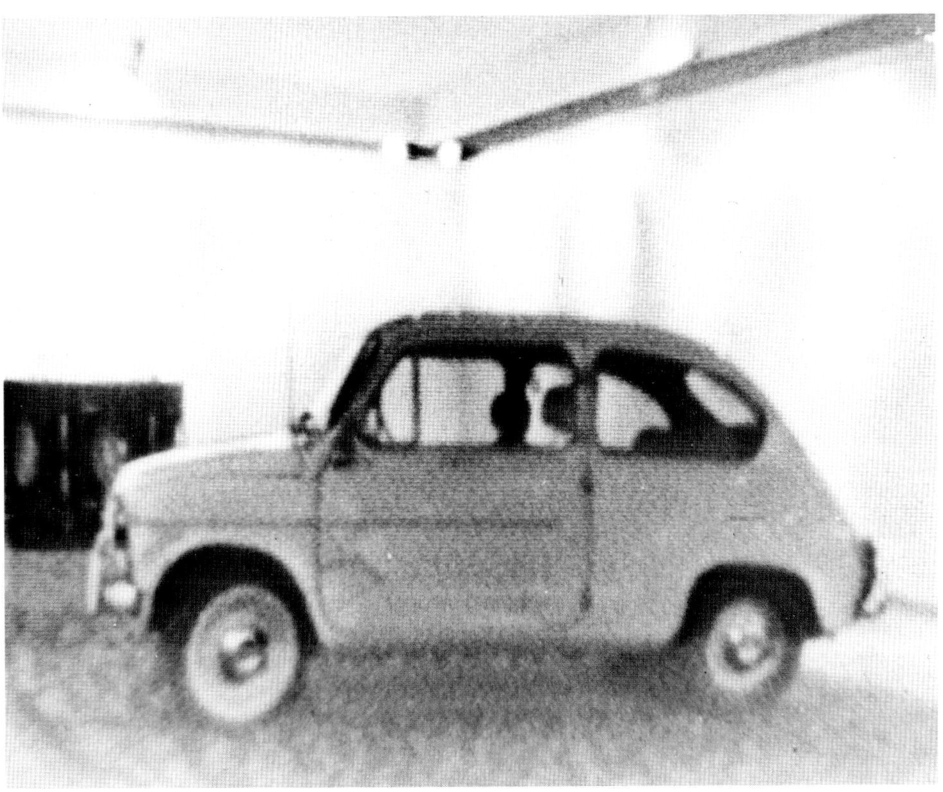

My First Car, 1972. At my request, a Catholic university museum bought a used 1961 Fiat for me to exhibit and own after the show. I needed a car, and for me this was a way for the church to support an artist as it did during the Italian Renaissance. DeSaisset Art Museum, University of Santa Clara, California.

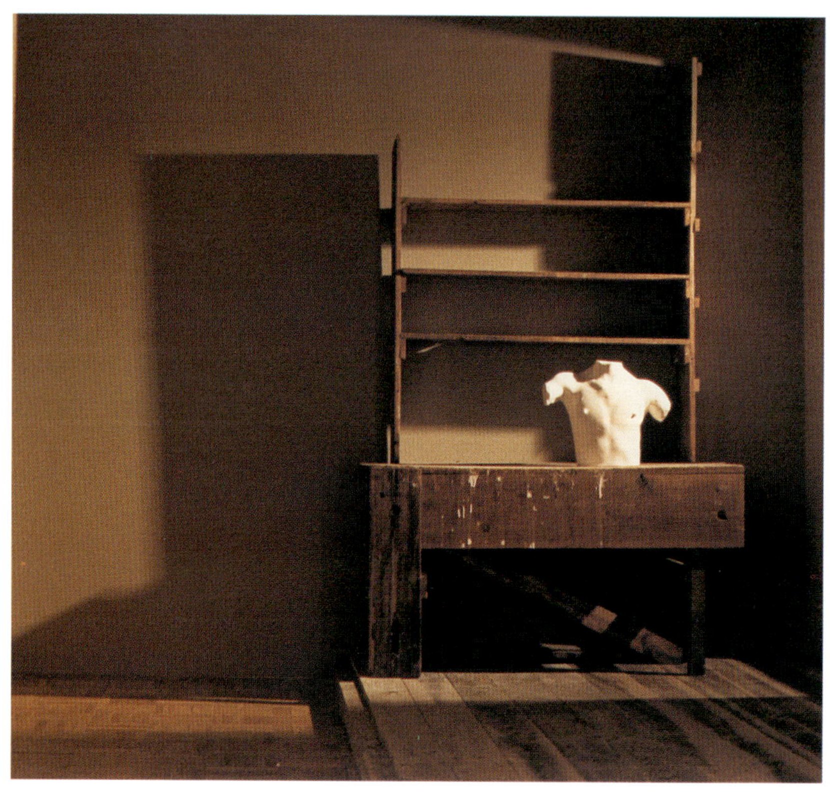

The Artist's Studio, 1973. Installation. Wood, plaster. 7×10×15'. Exhibited in *One Hundred Years of California Sculpture,* Oakland Art Museum, California.

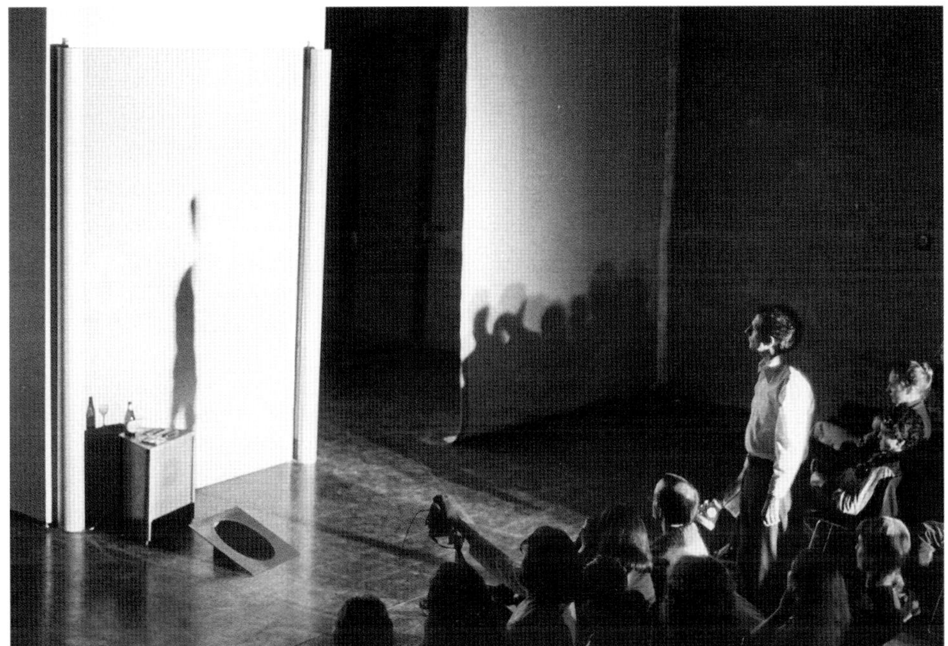

Studio Berkeley, 1980. Shadow drawing action with sound. University Art Museum, Berkeley, California.

Review

The Chicago Tribune January 23, 1981. Alan G. Artner. Museum of Contemporary Art.

…"Studio," a piece presented in Switzerland (1979) and California (1980), but modified here. It is first a tableau whose props suggest Marioni's place of work. Bathed in yellow — traditionally a color symbolizing enlightenment and the intellect — the space is filled with the artist's presence. A large sheet of paper is affixed to the rear wall, upon which Marioni casts an attenuated shadow. Behind the paper are two contact microphones that pick up the sound of the artist's pencil rhythmically filling in the shadow.…As Marioni relaxes, the pencil stroke is determined by the rhythm of his body. Twice during the 20 minute piece, this toccata-like pulse becomes counterpoint, first to Miles Davis' trumpet solo from "On Green Dolphin Street," then to Hayden's "Opus 1 Adagio for String Quartet." It also is interrupted as Marioni opens and pours a bottle of beer and later moves from the shadow to a parallelogram of light — the reflection of a tilted mirror. At that point one perceives the overriding plan, for Marioni is setting down a record of the artist at work: the shadow exerts its presence by filling and transforming its opposite, the "empty" circle of light. Once the creative process is complete, the artist exits in the artwork. Because of the placement of Marioni's two spotlights, each casting a shadow of half the body, he can withdraw behind a narrow curtain, seeming to disappear into the Giacometti-like self portrait. So the piece ends as it began, with the artist's presence filling the studio, but now not only through props.…Friday's act provided a multileveled experience whose poetry carried it far beyond most performances I have seen.

The Sound of Flight, 1977. Installation of drum brush drawings. M. H. DeYoung Memorial Museum, San Francisco.

I made my first drum brush drawings in 1972 and I continue to make these drawings, which are inspired by the automatic writings of the surrealist movement. The drawings are the result of rubbing and beating with steel wire drum brushes (like jazz drummers use) against a large sheet of sandpaper. The steel is transferred to the paper over a long period of time and the brushing on the sandpaper makes a rasping sound. The action is repetitive like that of a knife against a sharpening stone. The left hand makes a single arc, up and down, while the right hand moves in a circle-like motion in the shape of a violin or an artist's palette. Over the years the drawings have changed only slightly, like handwriting changes as personality evolves. This becomes a kind of talking-drumming, played on a hollow-core drawing board. The result is a pictorial record of the sound activity, a marriage of art and music. During a drawing/drumming session, because of the repetition of sound and action a trance state can occur and I can see elements of fantasy in the marks. To most people the results look like birds flying to the left.

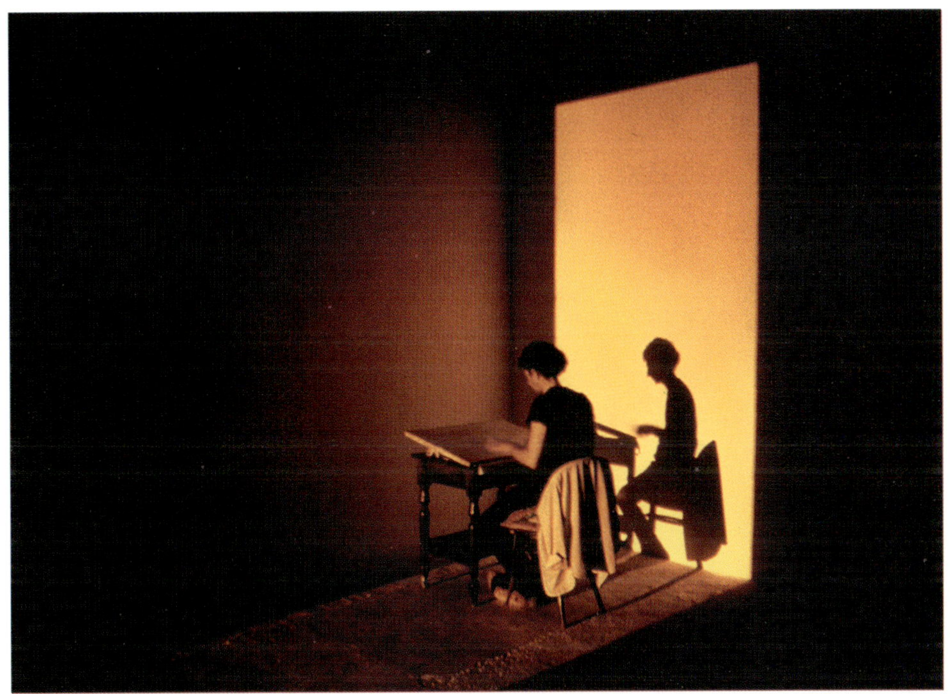

Liberating Light and Sound, 1979. Pellegrino Gallery, Bologna, Italy. A yellow light framed my drum-brushing action on a slab of marble. The marble became polished and the brushes became sharpened after the hour-long wire-brushing action.

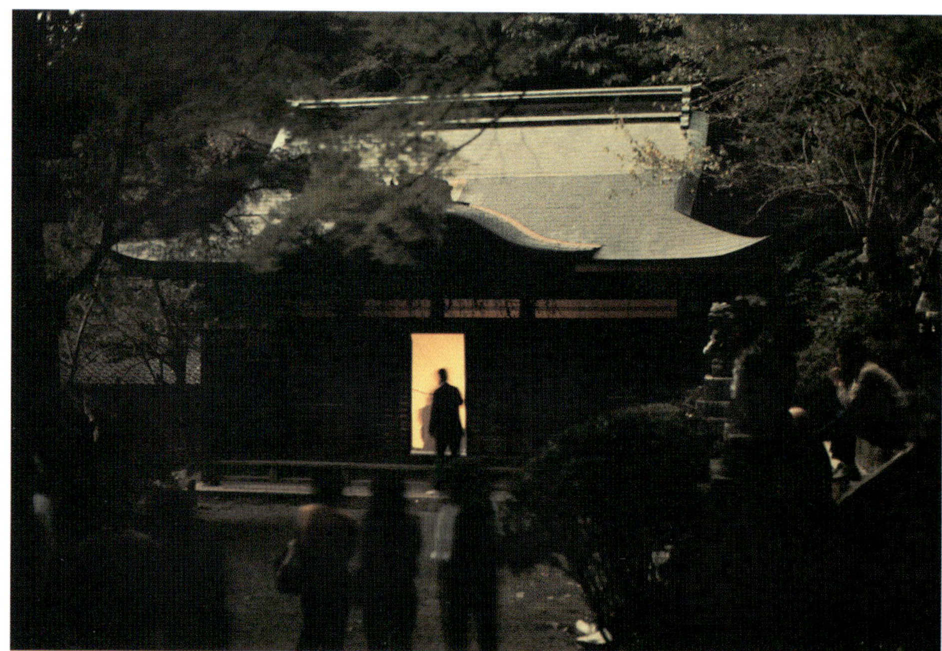

Studio Kyoto, 1982. Ohara Shrine, Kyoto, Japan. Sponsored by Belca House, Kyoto. As the sun went down at the Shinto shrine, a woman played the koto inside, with a candle behind her creating her shadow on paper stretched across the entrance and fitted with a microphone. I stood outside and, with a long pencil, filled in the shadow, creating percussive sounds and bending my body to follow the movement of the shadow. The audience stood outside under the trees, surrounded by smaller shrines and statues. This was a performance of merging opposites: light and dark, Eastern and Western, male and female, inside and outside.

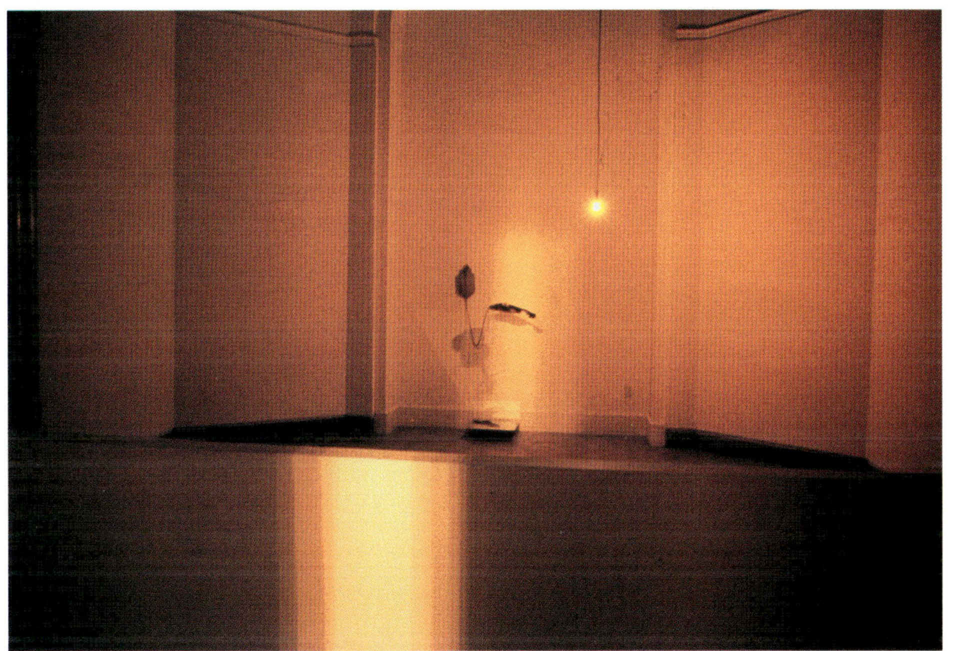

The Power of Suggestion (for Vienna), 1979. Installation, Modern Art Gallery, Vienna, Austria.

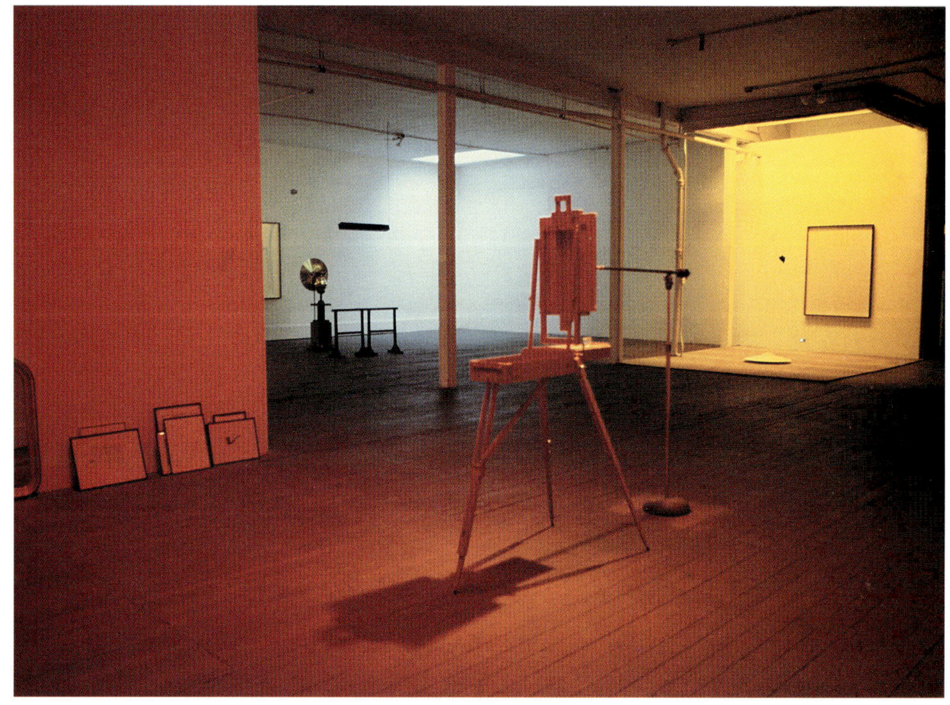

Paris, San Francisco, Kyoto, 1981. Installation. Site Inc. Gallery, San Francisco.

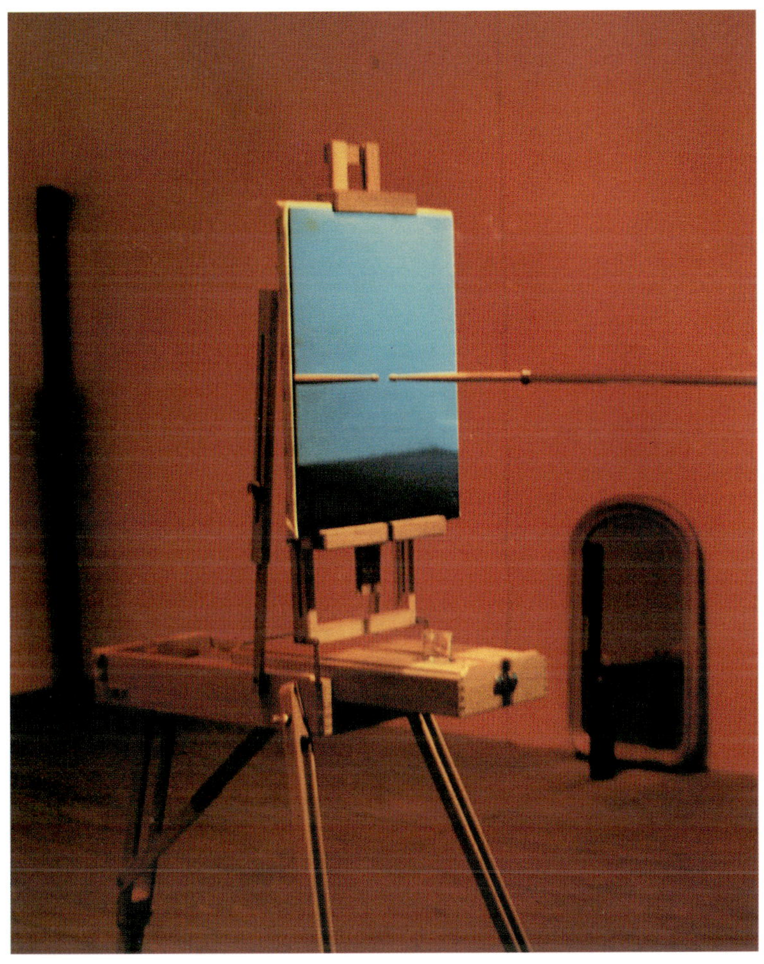

Paris, 1981. Installation. Site Inc. Gallery, San Francisco.

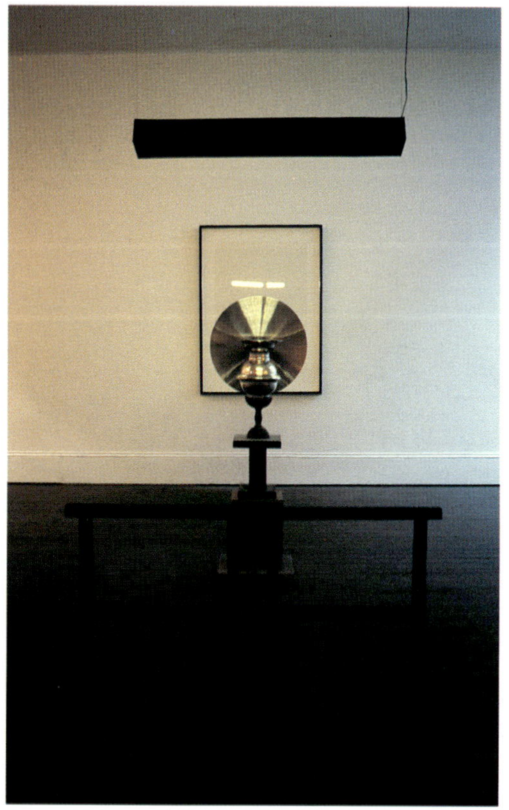

San Francisco, 1981. Installation. Site Inc. Gallery, San Francisco.

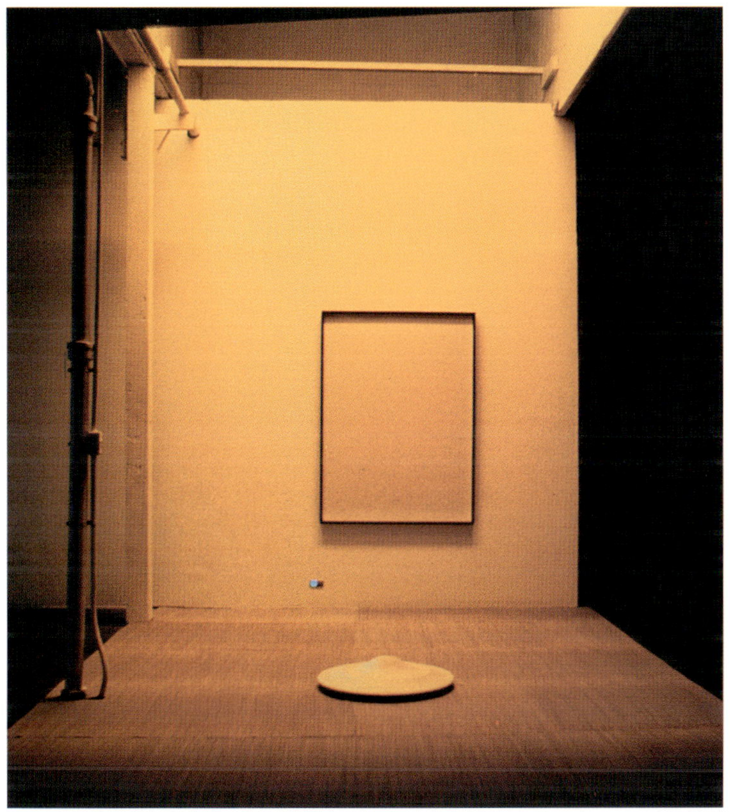

Kyoto, 1981. Installation. Site Inc. Gallery, San Francisco.

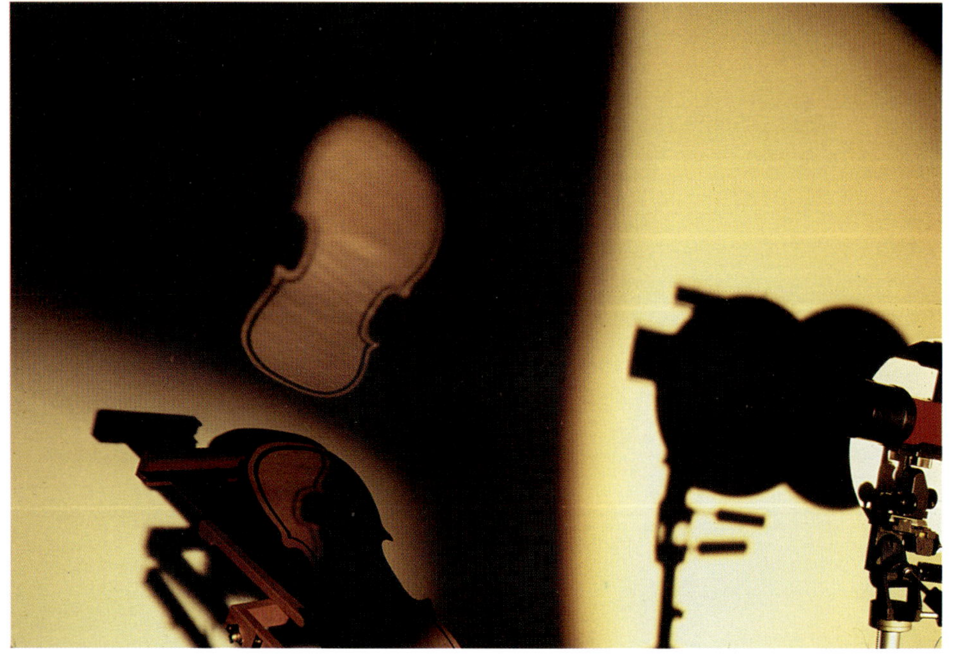

The Marriage of Art and Music for Los Angeles, 1985. Detail.

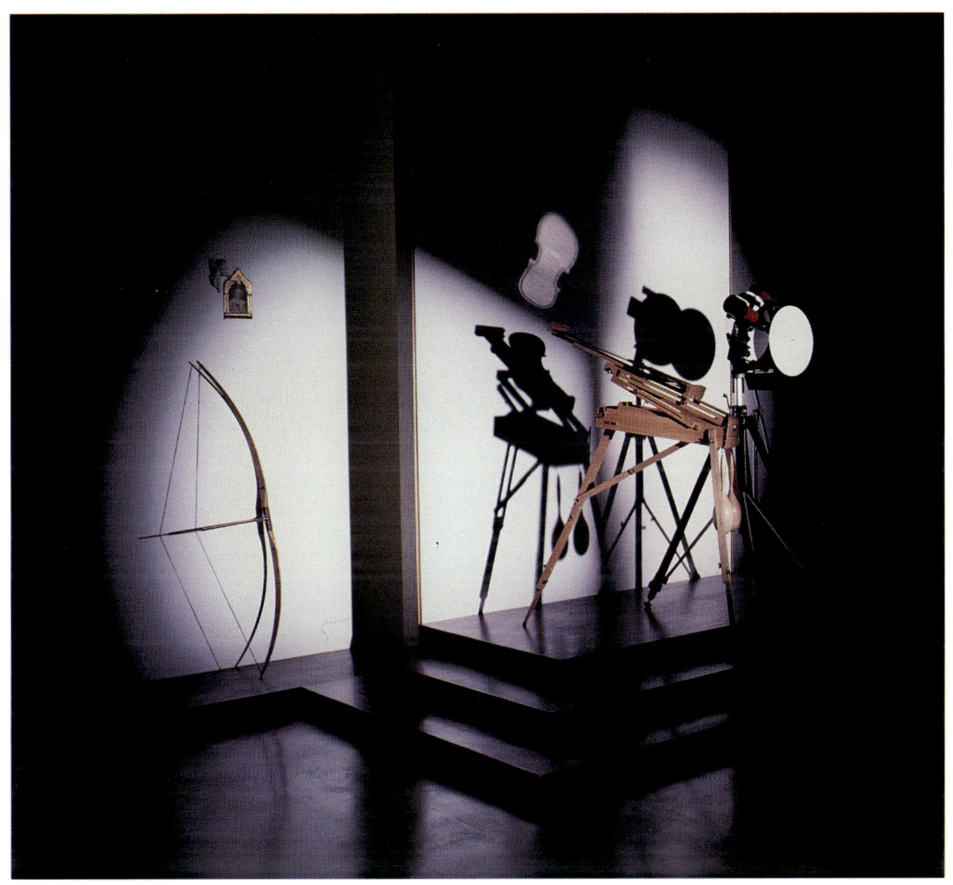

The Marriage of Art and Music for Los Angeles, 1985. Installation. Objects with light and shadow. For the New Music America Festival, Otis Art Institute, Los Angeles.

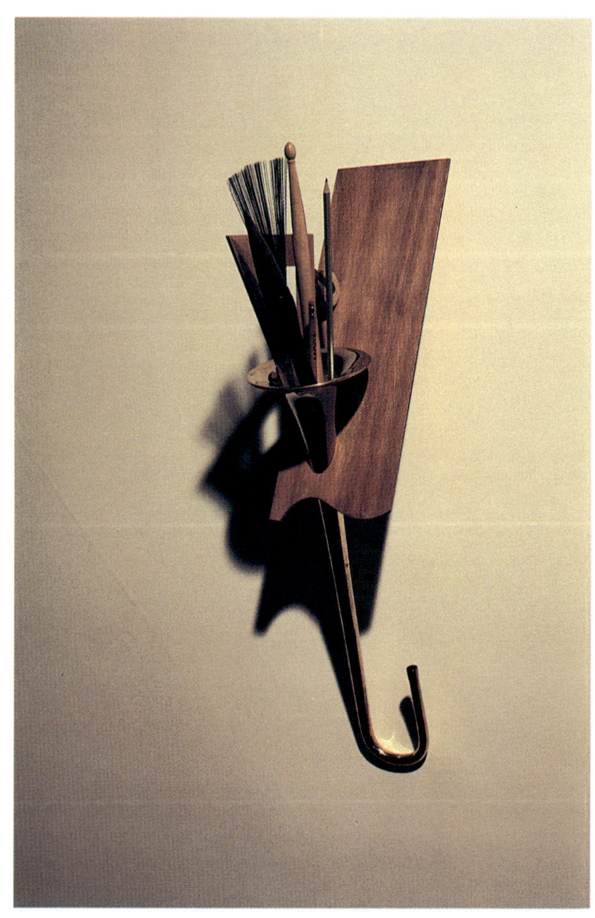

The Bride's Bouquet, 1985. Sculpture, wood, brass, with objects. 18×7×5". Private collection, San Francisco.

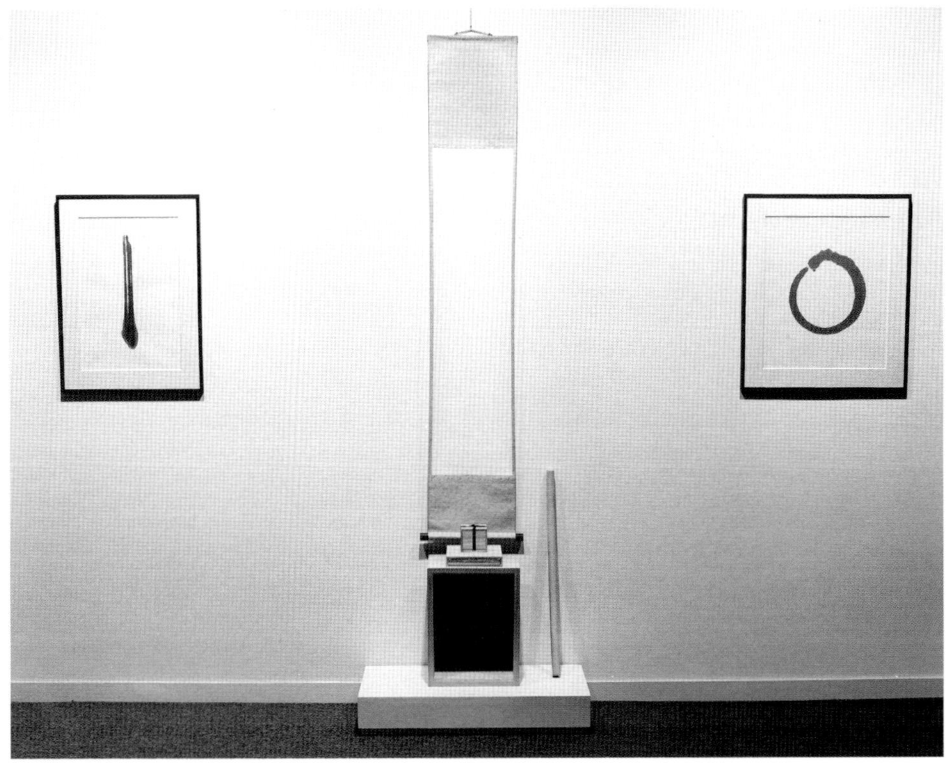

The Japanese, Part I, 1987. Tableau sculpture. 8×10×2'. Objects with two framed draw-ings, ink on linen.

The Germans, Part 1, 1986. Two part sculpture (with The Italians). Tableau sculpture with objects and a lithograph, 6×4×2'. Collection San Francisco Museum of Modern Art.

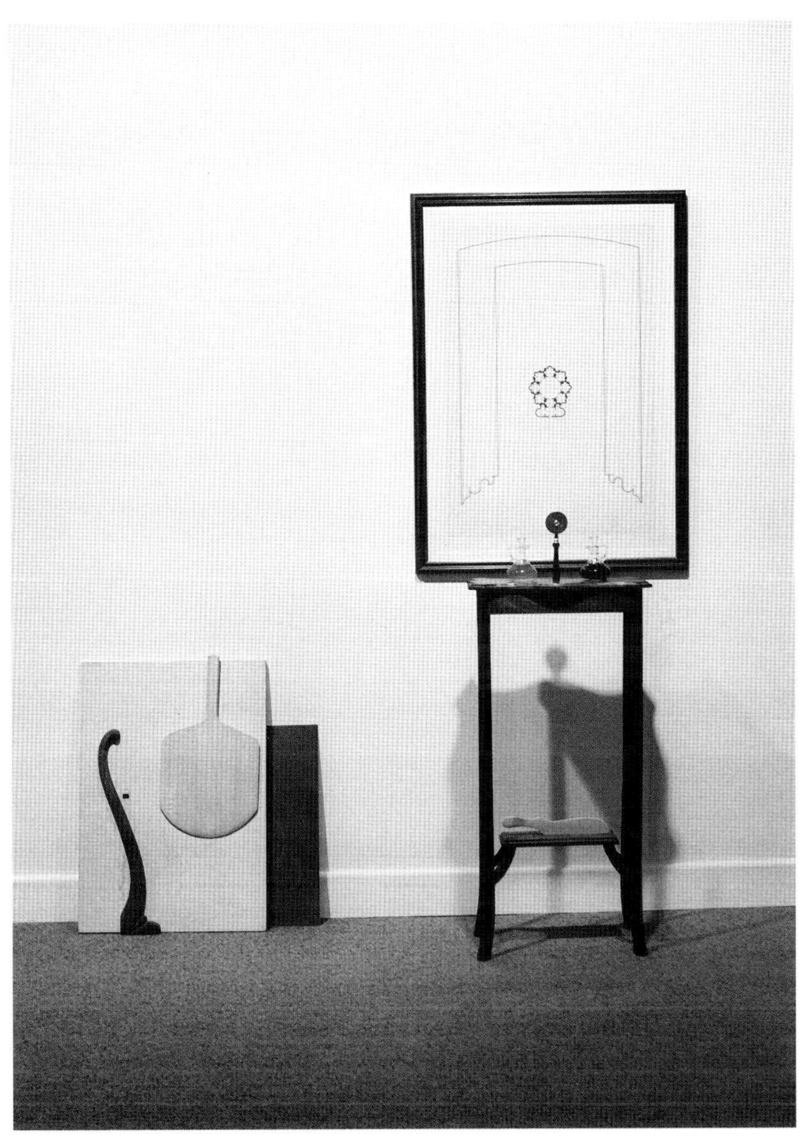

The Italians, Part I, 1986. Two part sculpture (with The Germans). Tableau sculpture with objects, lithograph and yellow light. 6×4×2', Collection San Francisco Museum of Modern Art.

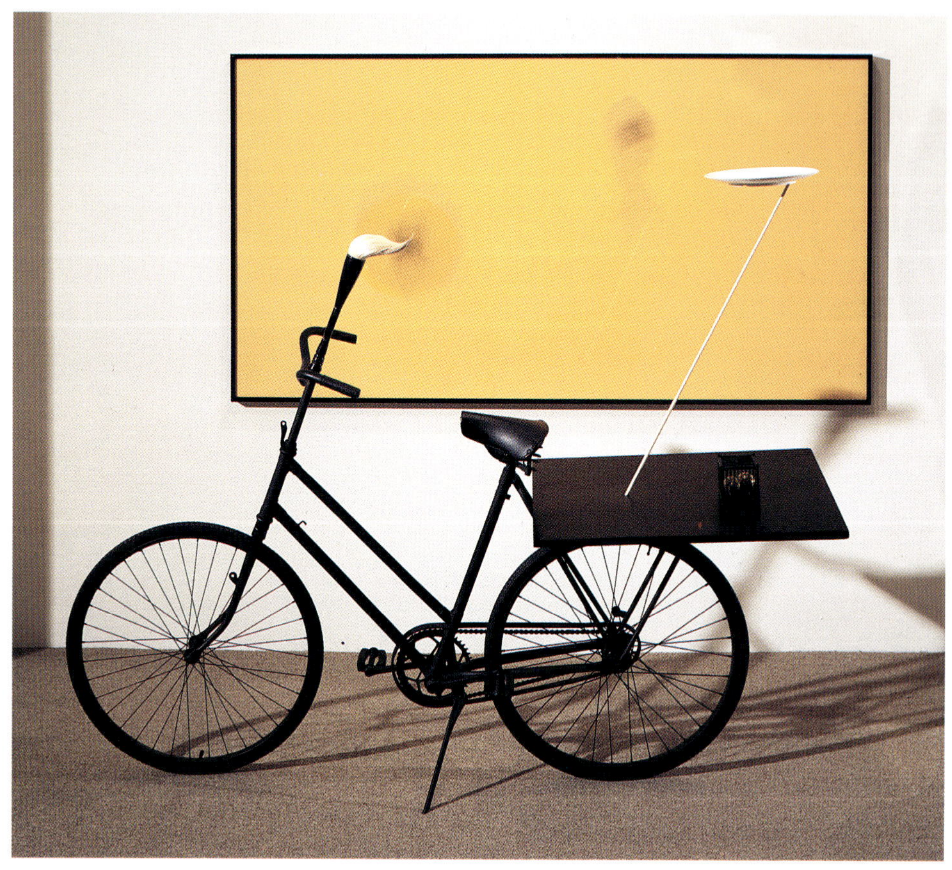

Beijing, 1989. Tableau sculpture, objects with drawing. 5×7×2'.

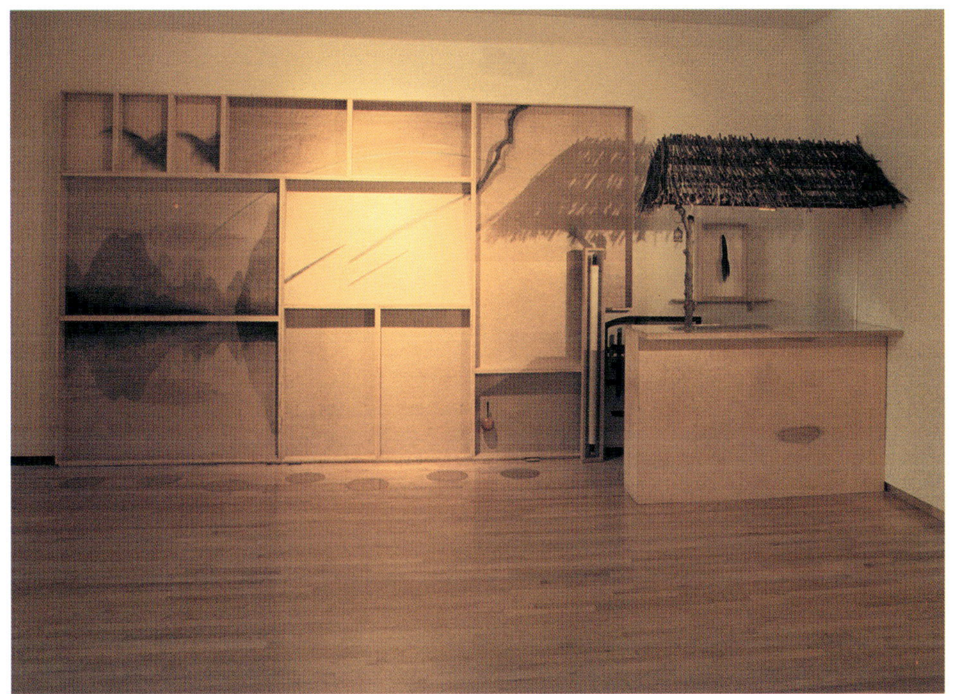

By the Sea (The Pacific Rim), 1992-93. Installation. 9×21×5'. Objects, light and shadow with drawings on wood. This installation includes a functioning bar open on Wednesdays as an interactive element.

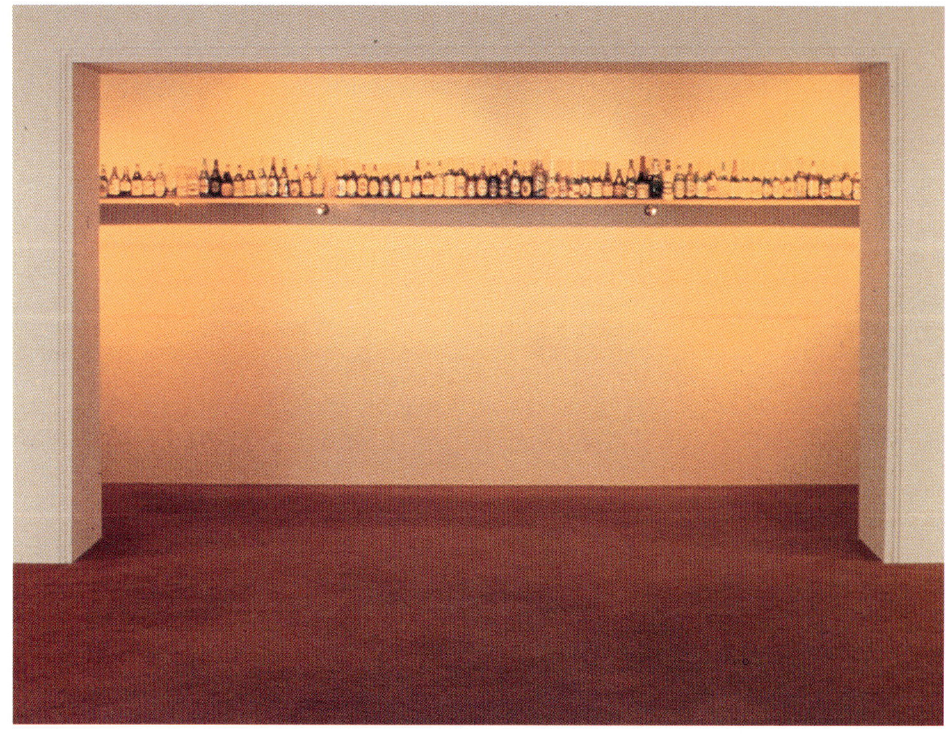

From China to Czechoslovakia, 1990. (First version, 1976). World map in beer bottles.

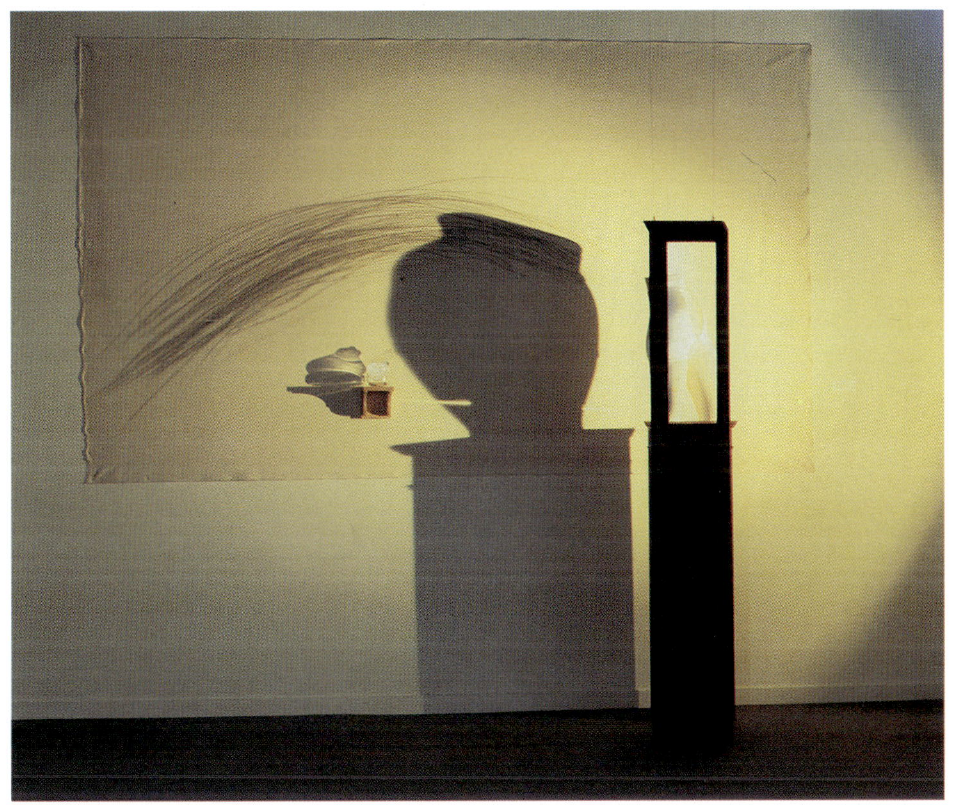

Room for Interpretation, 1987. Tableau sculpture. 8×8×3'. Objects, drawing on canvas, yellow light and shadow.

Notes on Public Sculpture

Sculpture is about the relationship of forms in space
It should grace the landscape
Not be symmetrical
Use the geometry of nature
Have good proportions
Be controversial at first
Become a thing of pride to the public
Have a subject
Make a point
Be symbolic of something
Not be generic abstract
It should be sensitive to where it is
Work with its neighboring objects
Emphasize local character
Have a social element
Use shadows
Be a spirit in the dark
It is an object that draws you to it
Has poetry or technological information
Predicts the future
Allows your imagination to travel to the past
It should bring people up to the level of art
Fight against a world of standardization
Have layers of meaning
Be open to interpretation
Not be painted red (a little red goes a long way)
It should have more than one side
Not emit obnoxious sounds
Consider acoustics
Reject vandalism
Encourage participation

1991

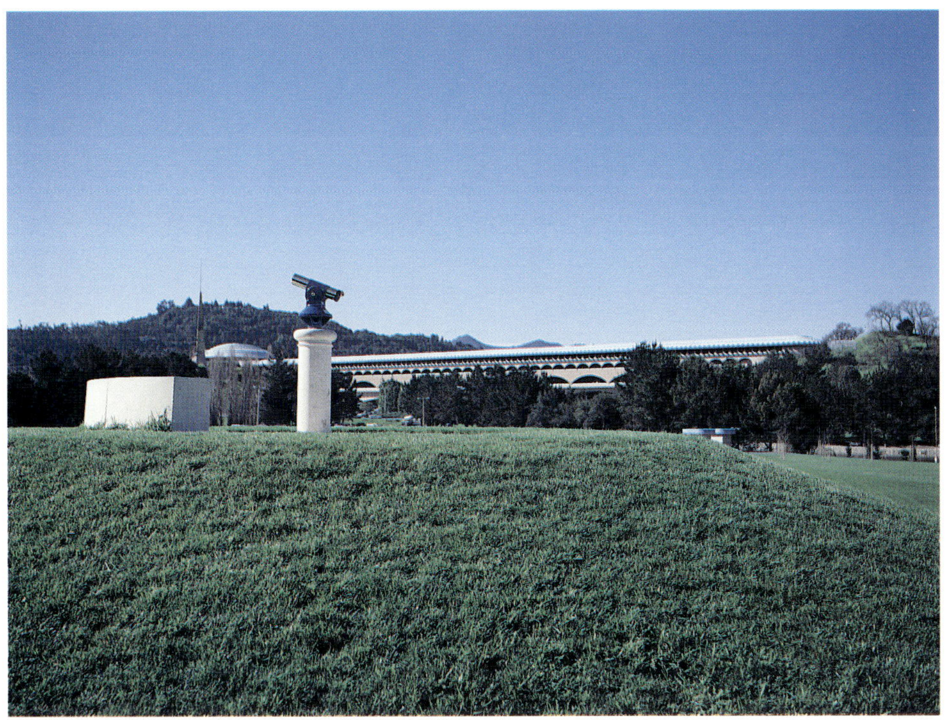

Observatory Bird, 1988. Marin County Civic Center. Public sculpture. 40' mound with functioning custom designed telescope. Sponsored by Public Artworks and the Marin County Department of Parks, Open Space and Cultural Affairs, San Rafael, California.

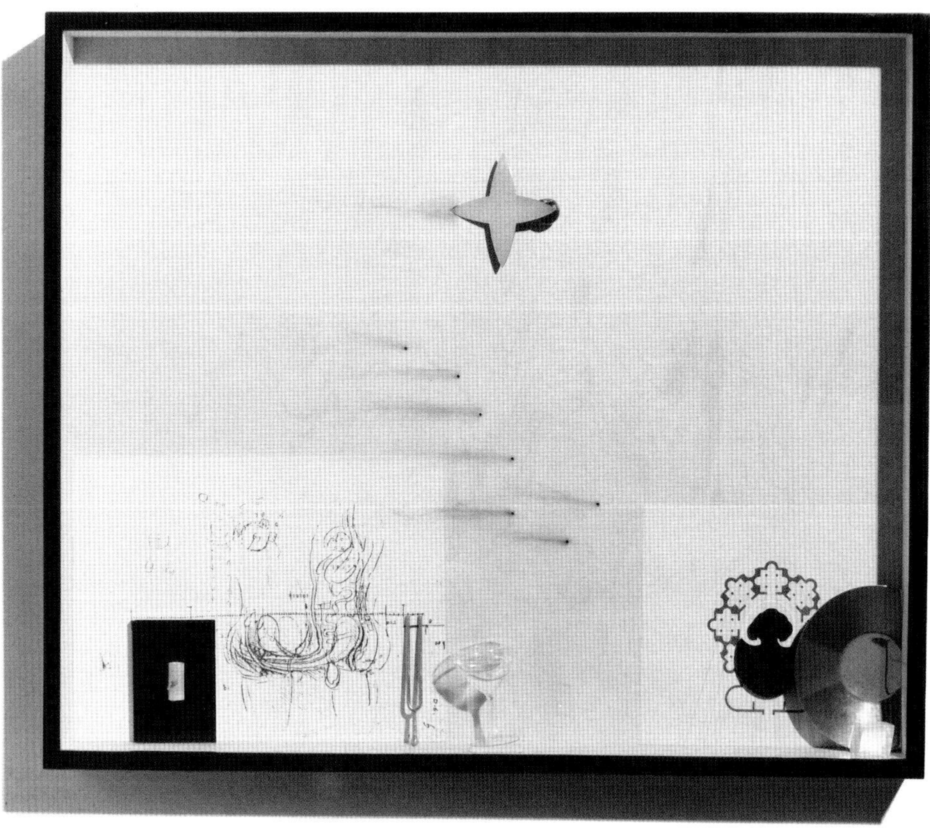

Sunday, 1989. Shadow box. Mixed media. 30×36×4". This is one of a series of 7 shadow boxes named for days of the week that make reference to the creation as described in the Bible.

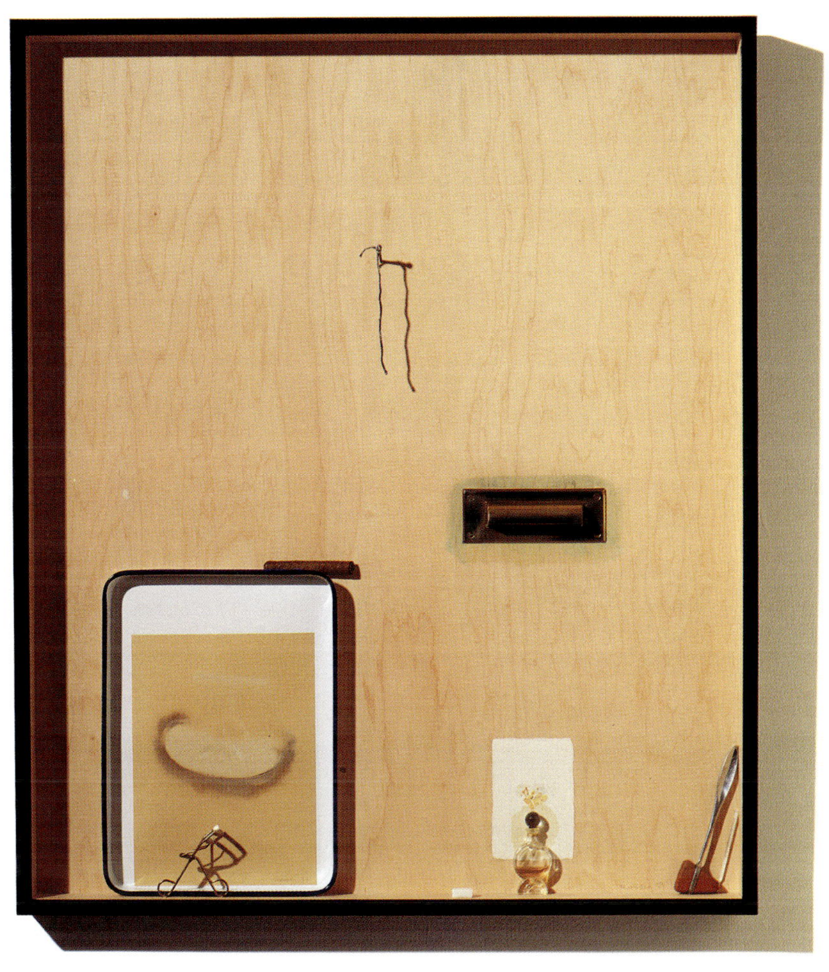

Monday, 1989. Shadow box. Mixed media. 42×36×4".

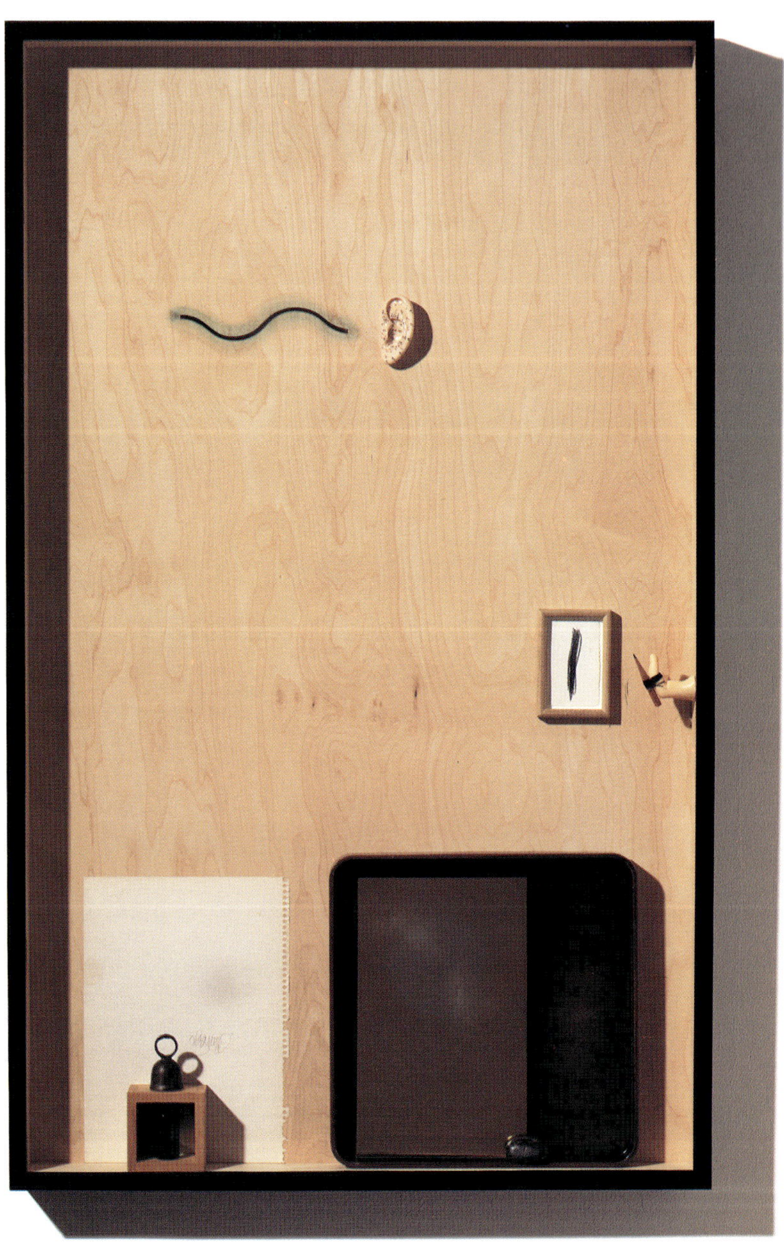

Tuesday, 1989. Shadow box. Mixed media. 48×30×4".

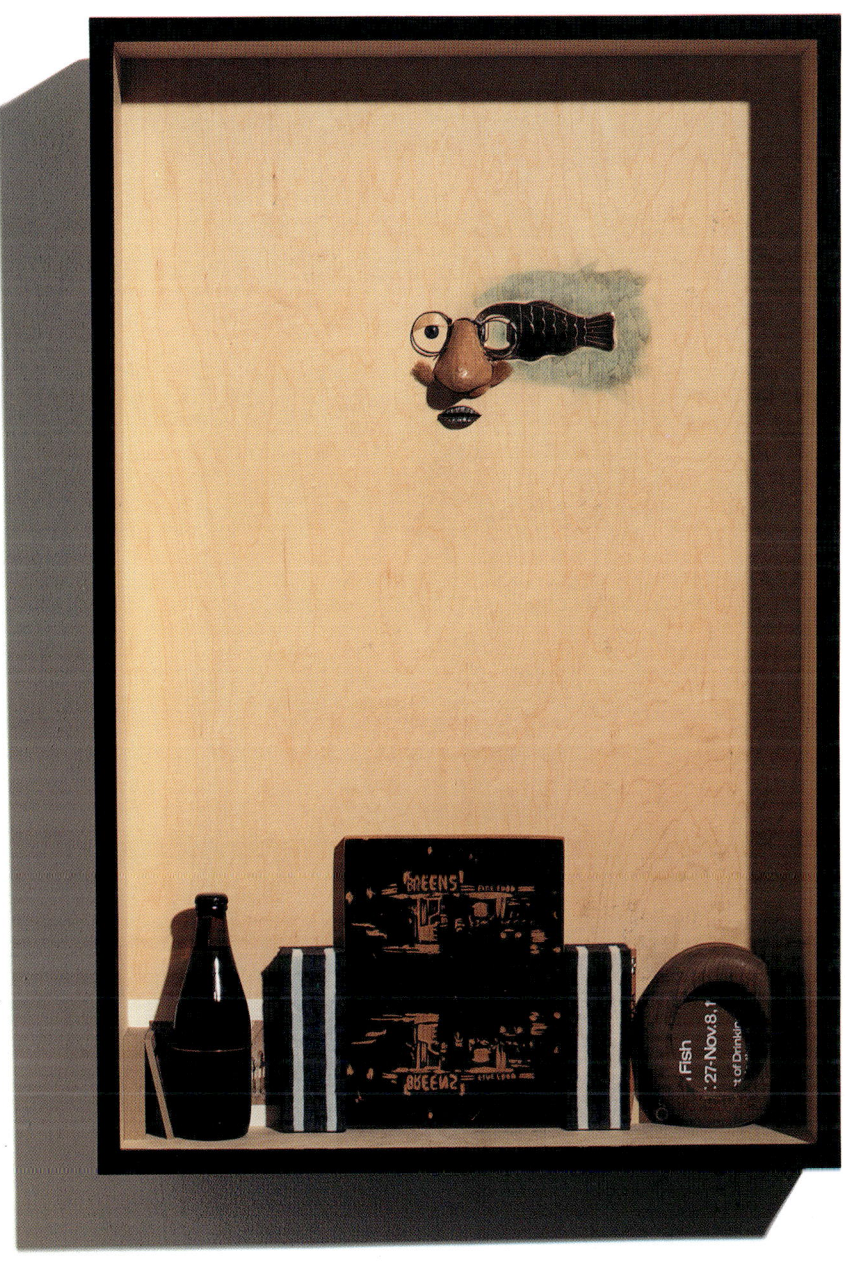

Wednesday, 1989. Shadow box. Mixed media. 36×24×4". Private collection, Honolulu, Hawaii.

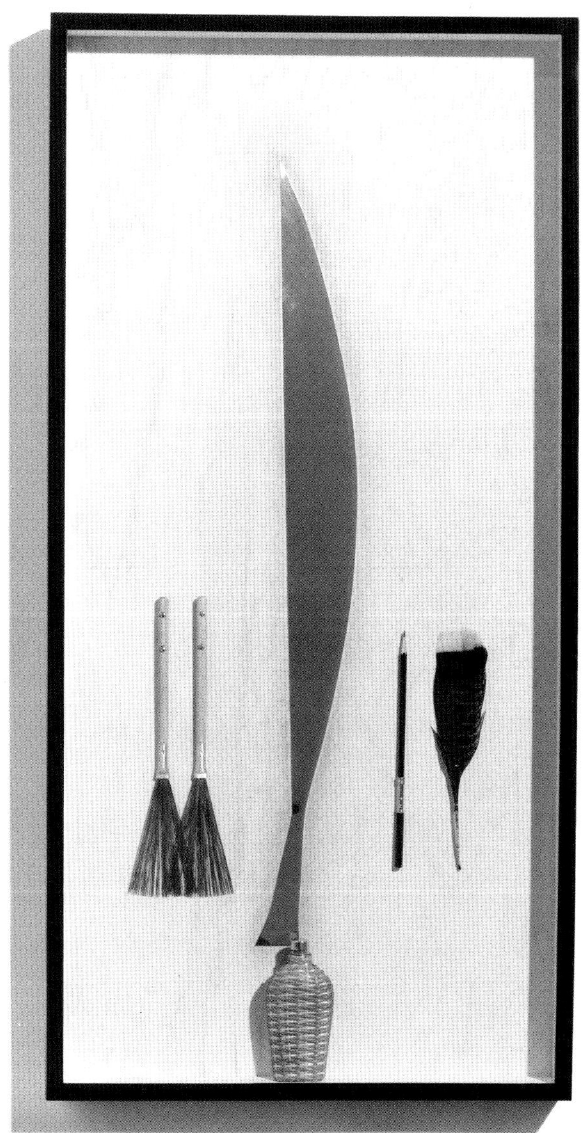

Thursday, 1989. Shadow box. Mixed media. 48×24×4".

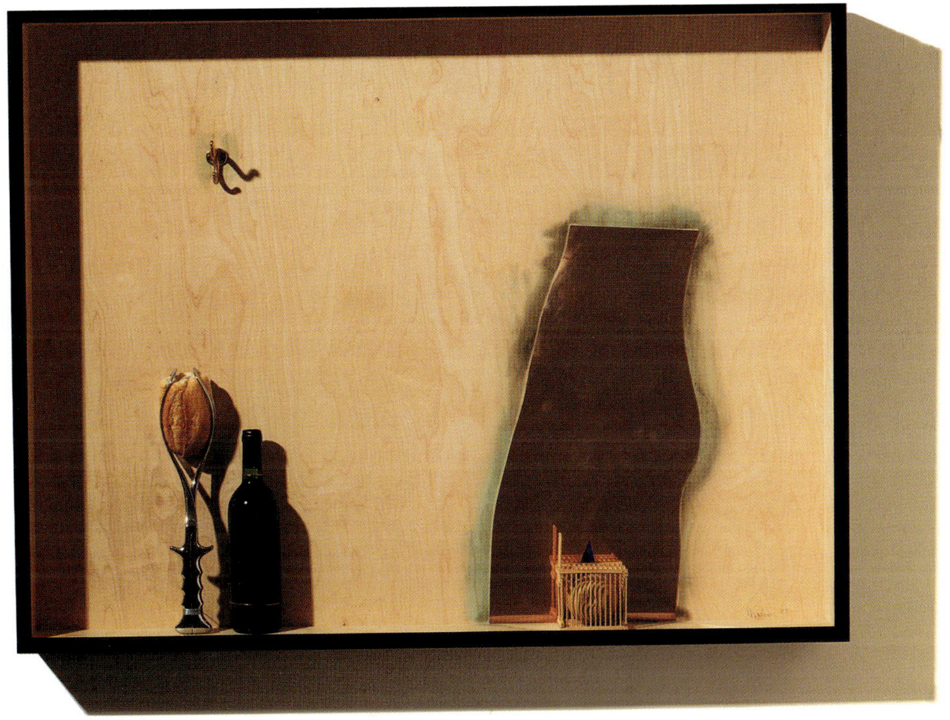

Friday, 1989. Shadow box. Mixed media. 36×48×4". Collection, diRosa Preserve, Napa, California.

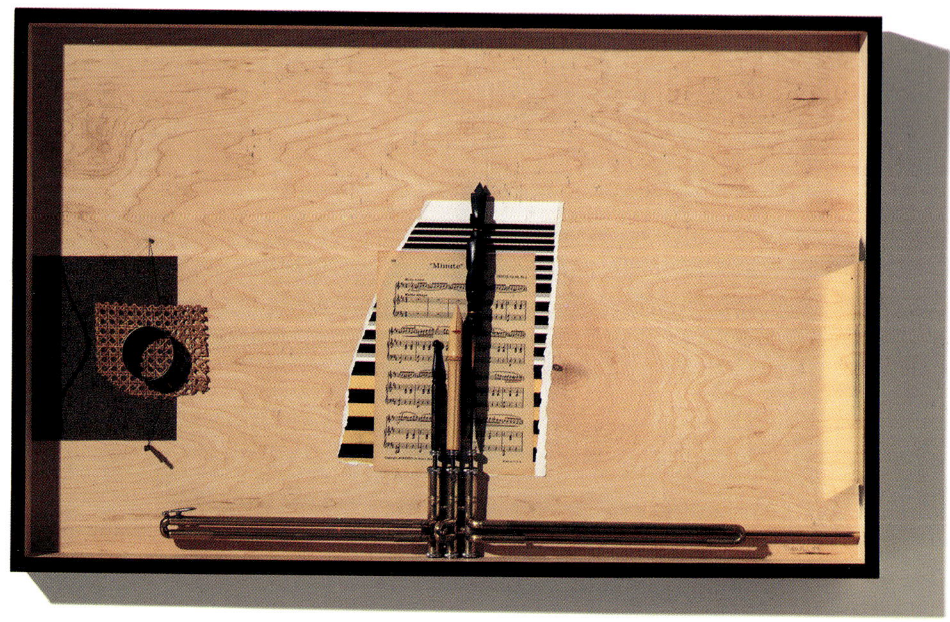

Saturday, 1989. Shadow box. Mixed media. 30×48×4".

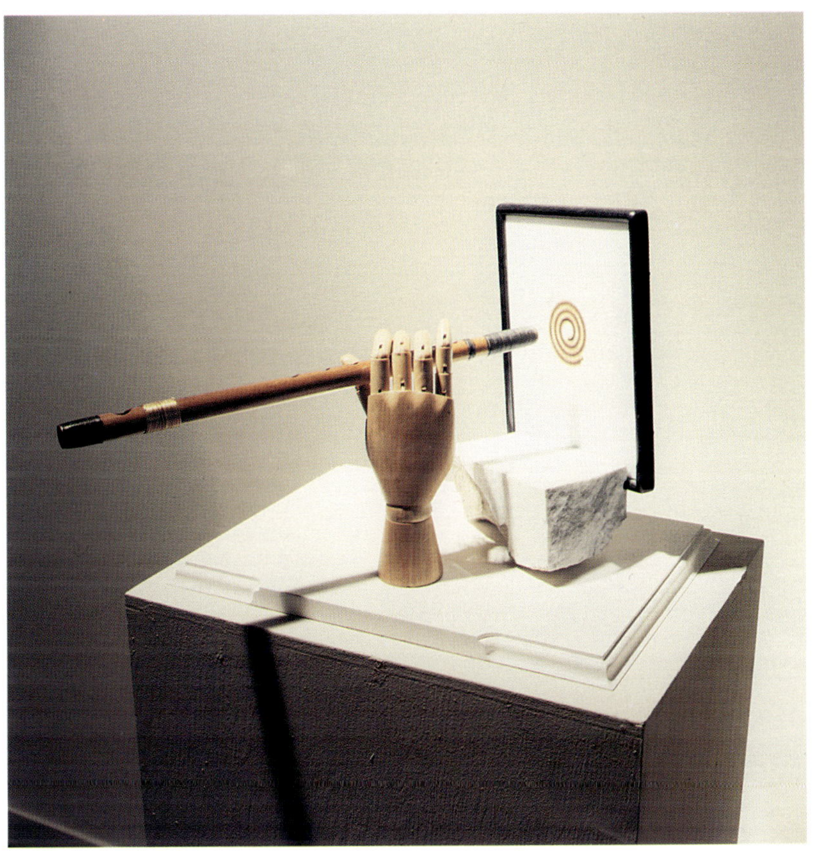

Bird in Hand, 1986. Sculpture, wood, bamboo flute, marble, framed drawing. 10×14×14". Private collection, Montreal, Canada.

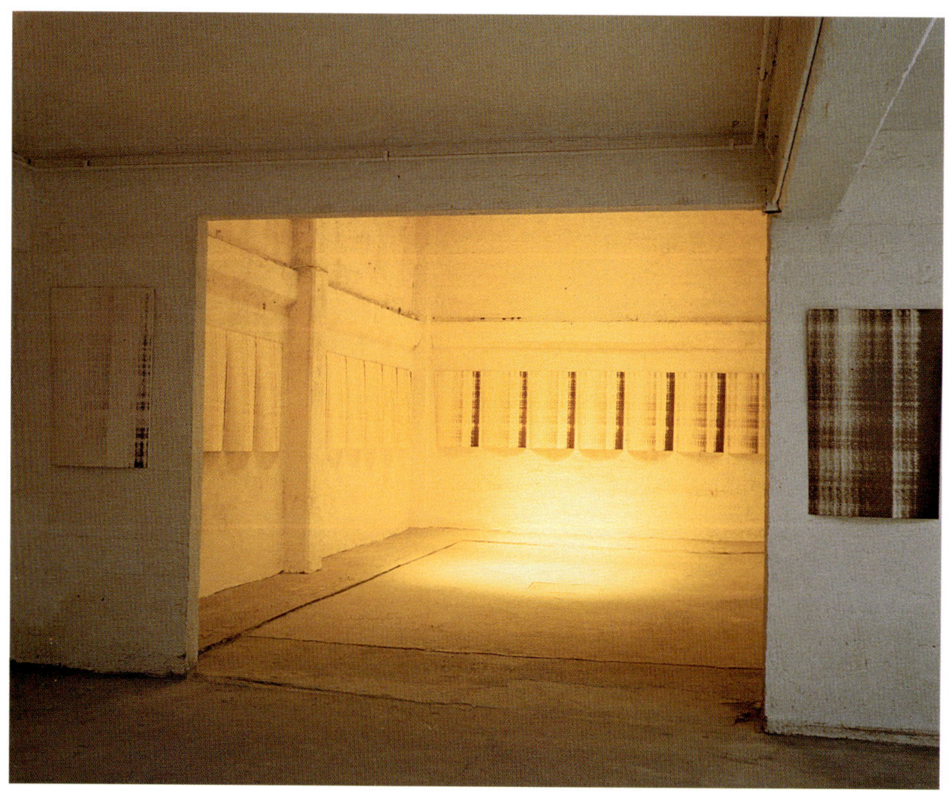

Process Print, 1990 (first version 1970). Installation of offset print with a copper panel on the floor and a yellow skylight. Capp Street Project, San Francisco.

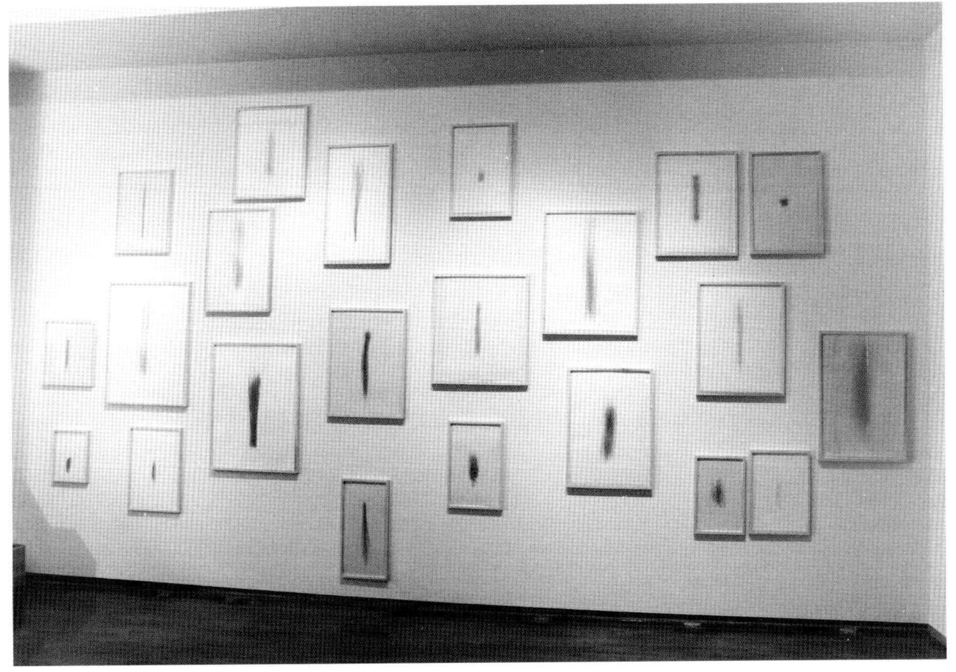

22 Line Drawings, 1995. Installation. 12×22'. Framed drawings. Pencil on paper. (Hung in the position they were made).

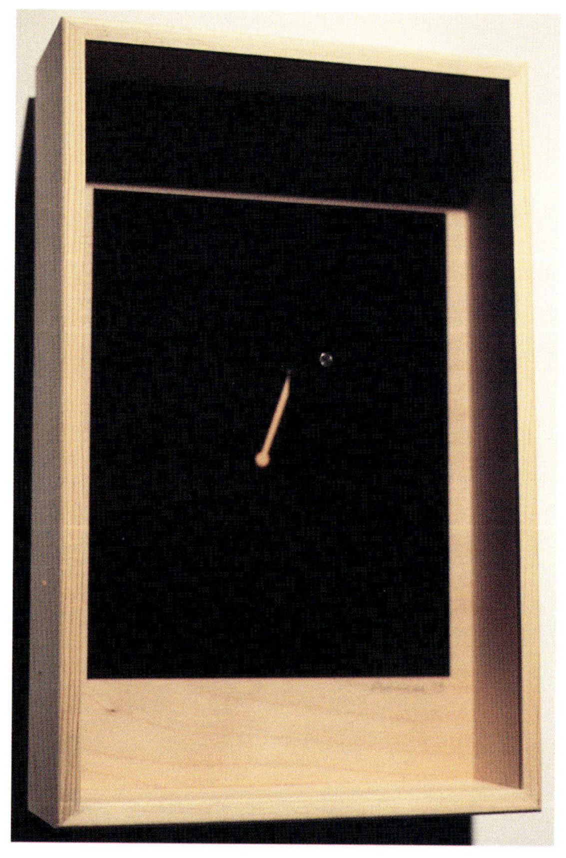

Nail, 1994. Shadowgram with its object. 15×10×4".

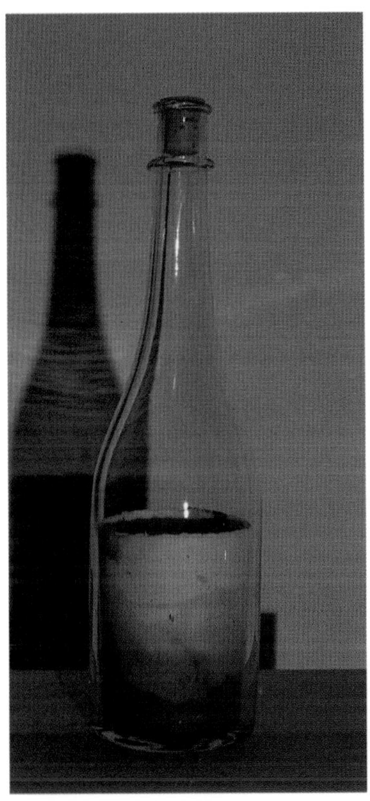

Bottled Landscape, 1992. Hand blown bottle containing an ink drawing made inside it. 13×4×4"

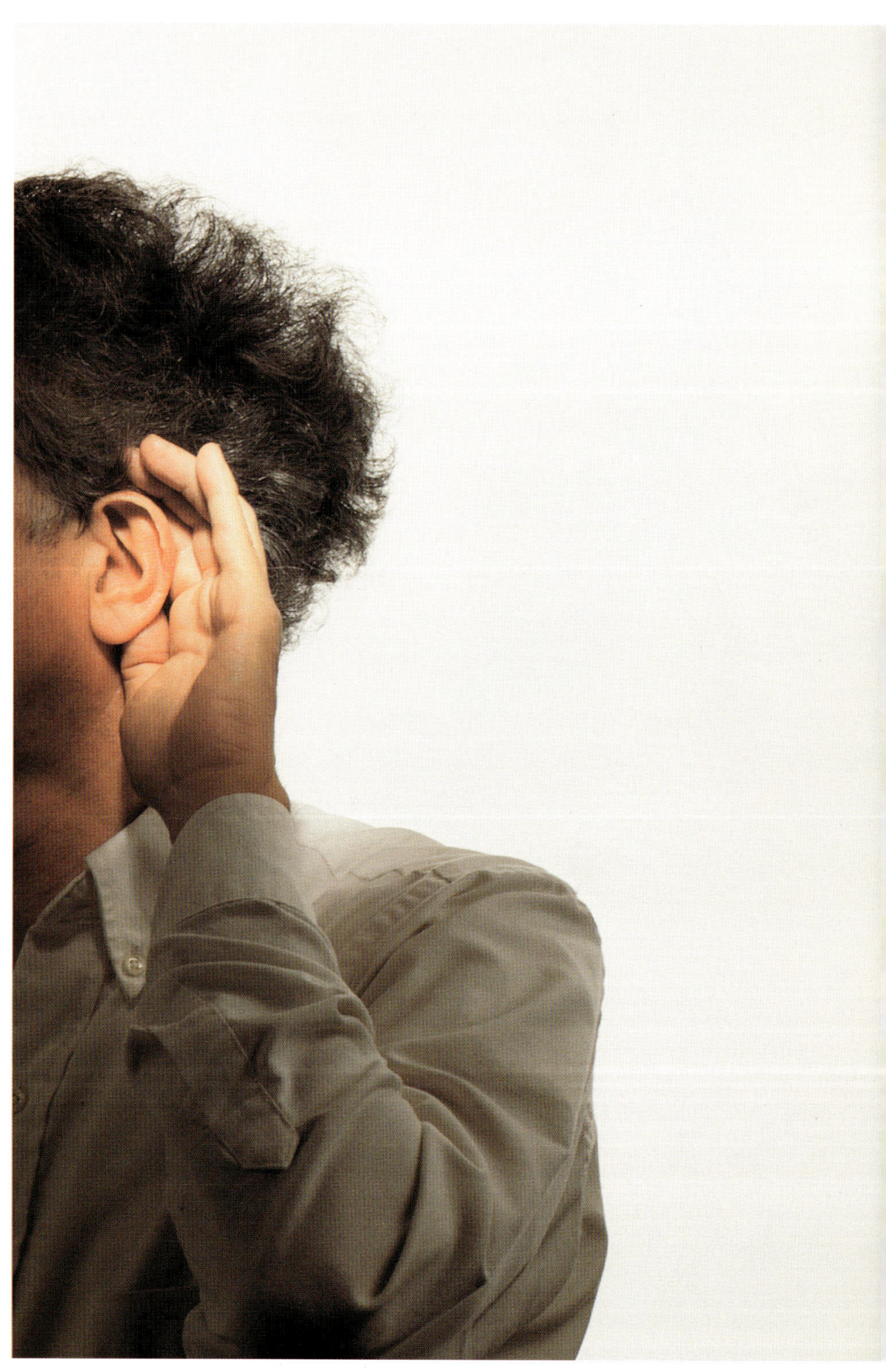

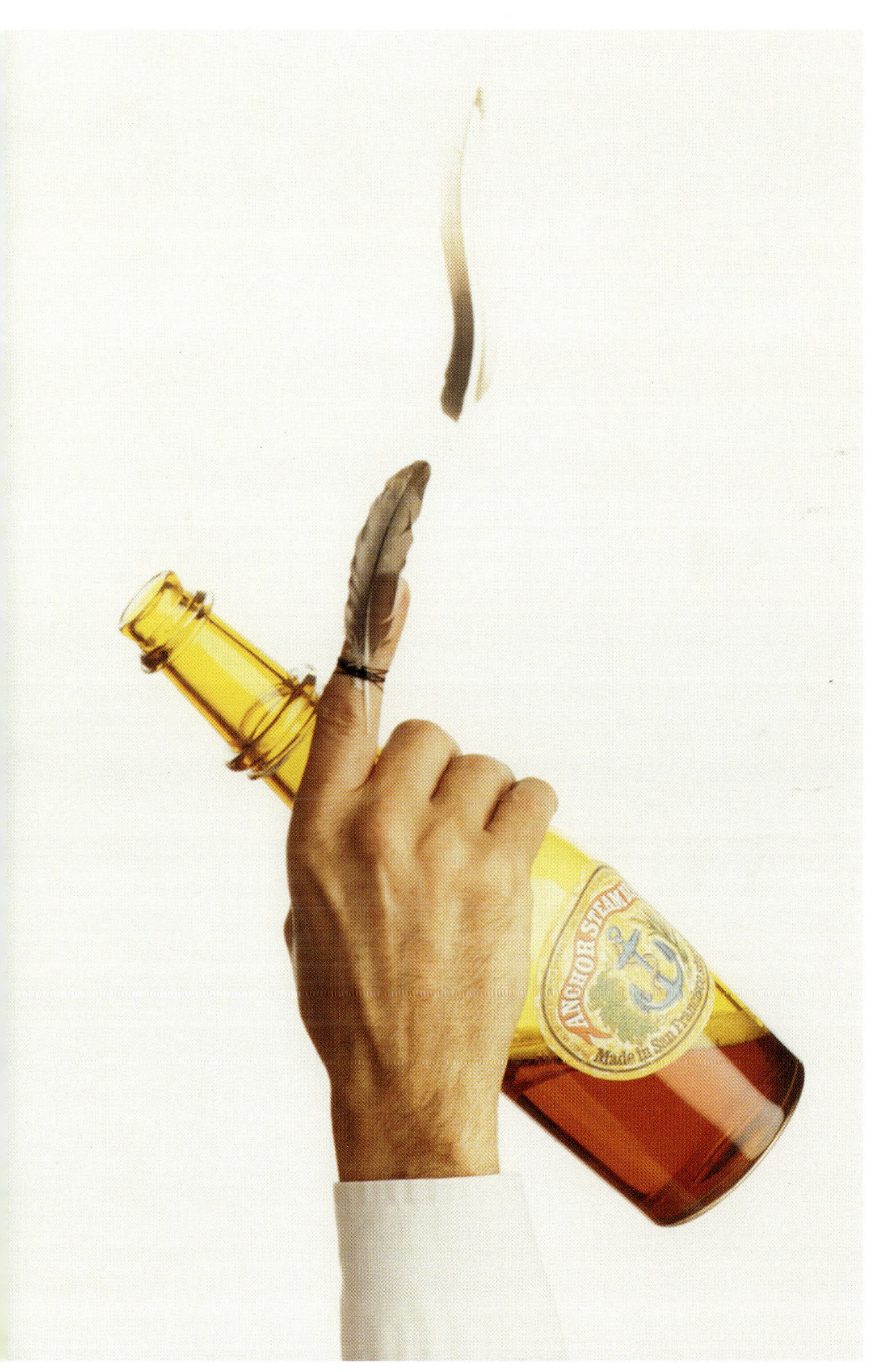

Project for Contemporania Magazine, January, 1991.

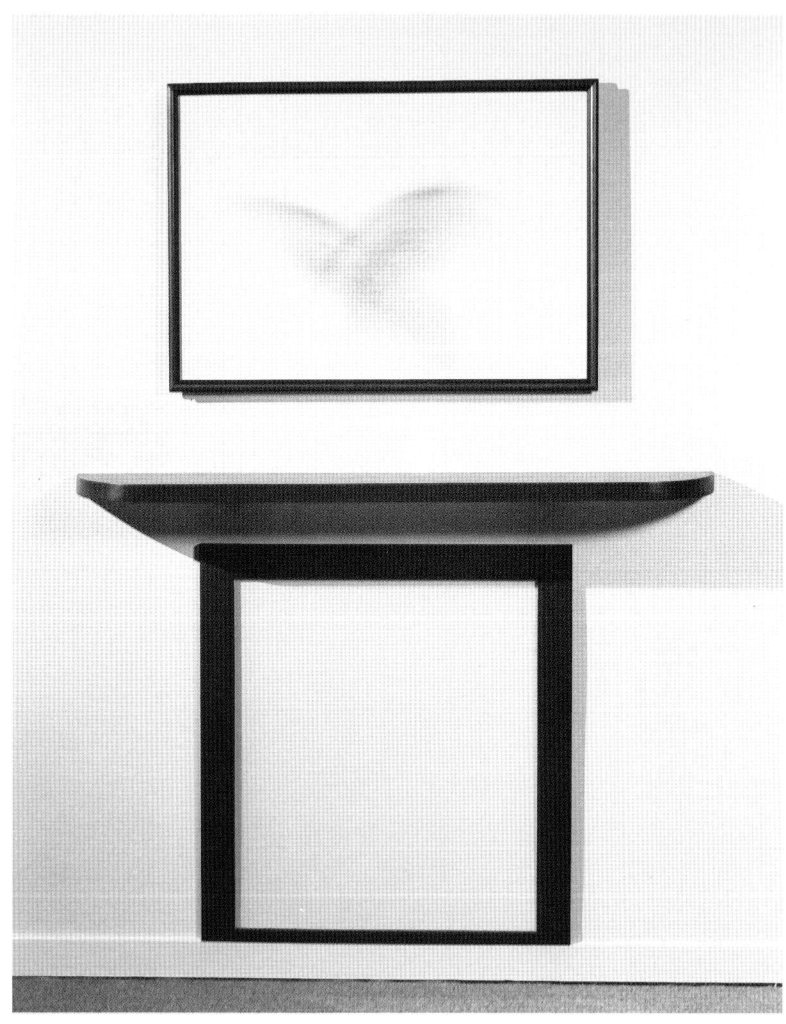

By the Fire, 1994. Tableau sculpture. 7×4×1'. Wood and framed drum brush drawing.

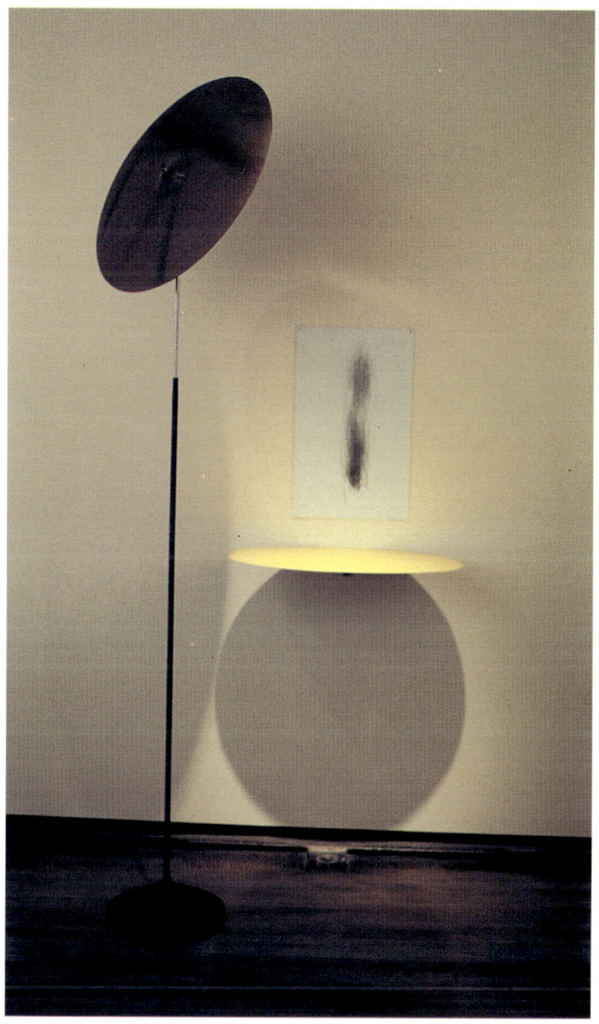

Illuminated Drawing, 1996. Tableau sculpture. 6'3"×3'8"×2'5". Pencil on painted copper, copper shelf painted with yellow enamel; brass cymbal, one spotlight, shadows, light reflection.

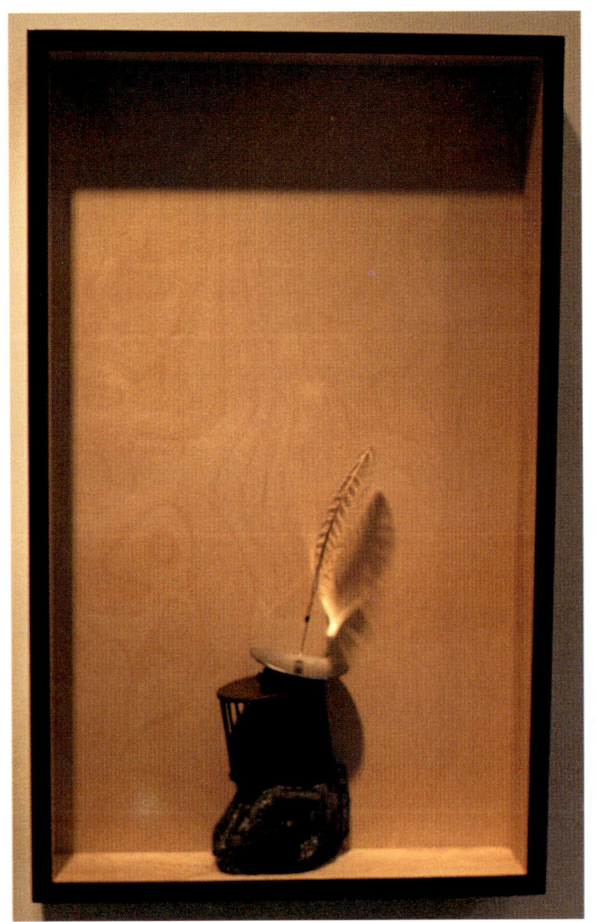

Lost at Sea, 1992. Shadow box. 33×20×4". Cricket cage, solar cigarette lighter, feather, rock, light reflection.

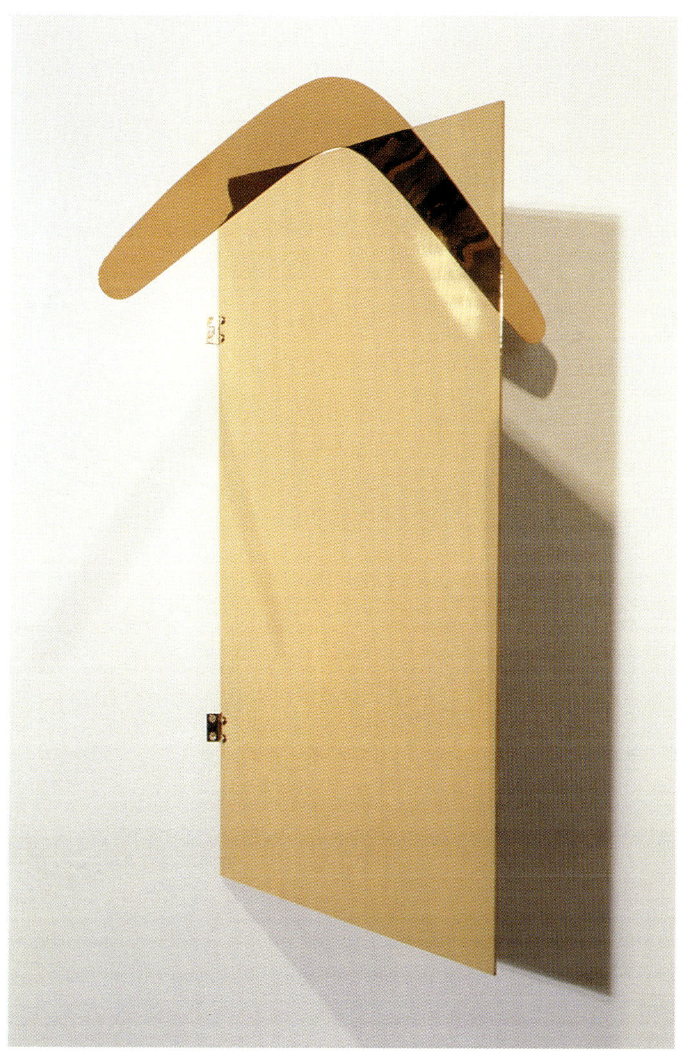

Golden Rectangle with Boomerang, 1987. Wall sculpture. Gold plated copper. 24×15×10". Private collection. San Francisco.

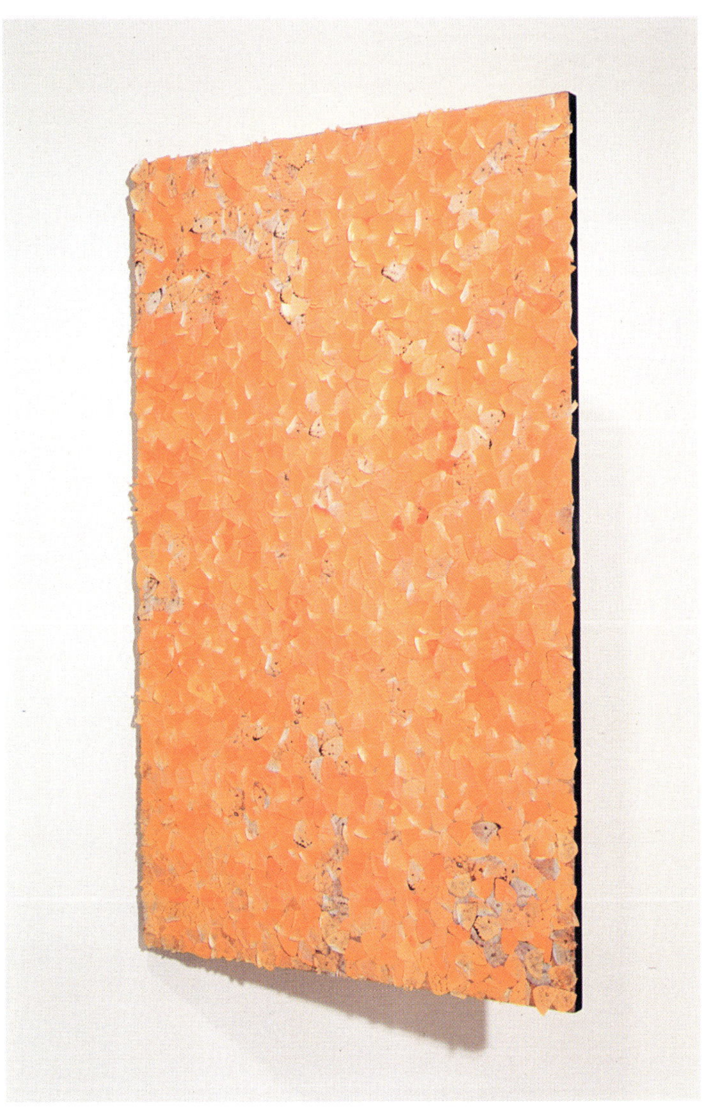

Golden Wing, 1988. Wall sculpture. Butterflies on wood with metal hinges. 33×20×5". Collection M. H. DeYoung Memorial Museum, San Francisco.

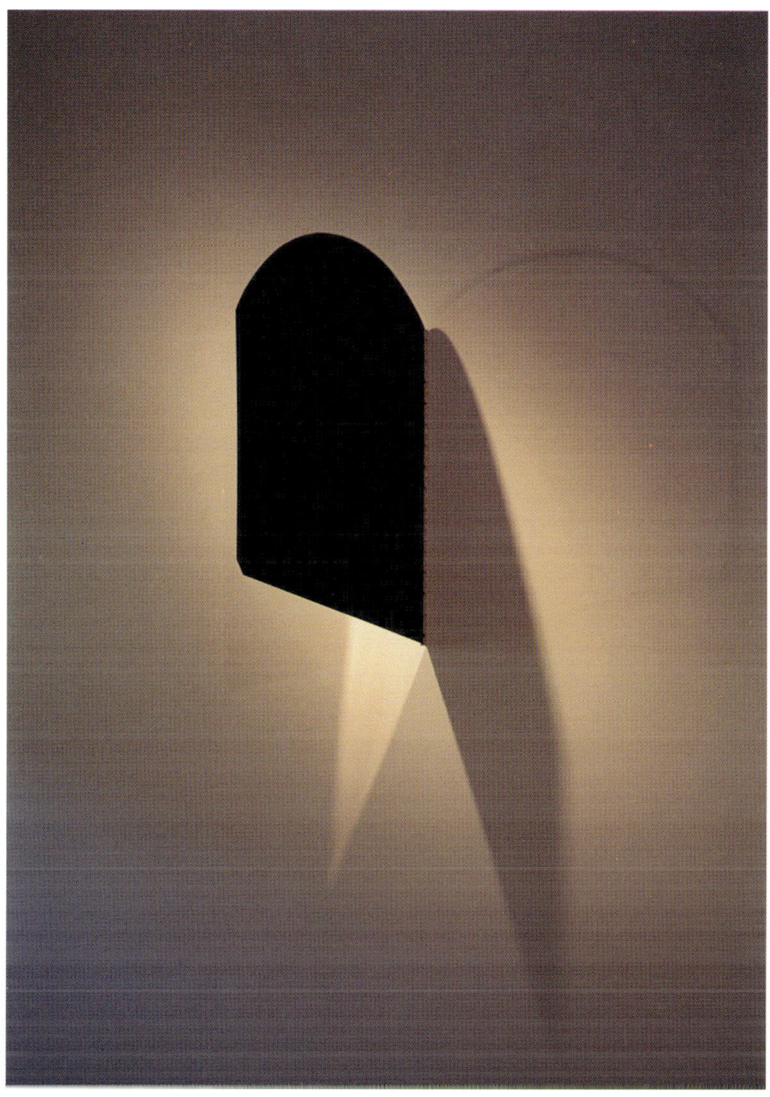

Circle, Triangle, Square, 1996. Wall sculpture. Copper painted black on one side and hinged to the wall. Light, shadow and a stain on the wall from metal polish. 3×4×2'.

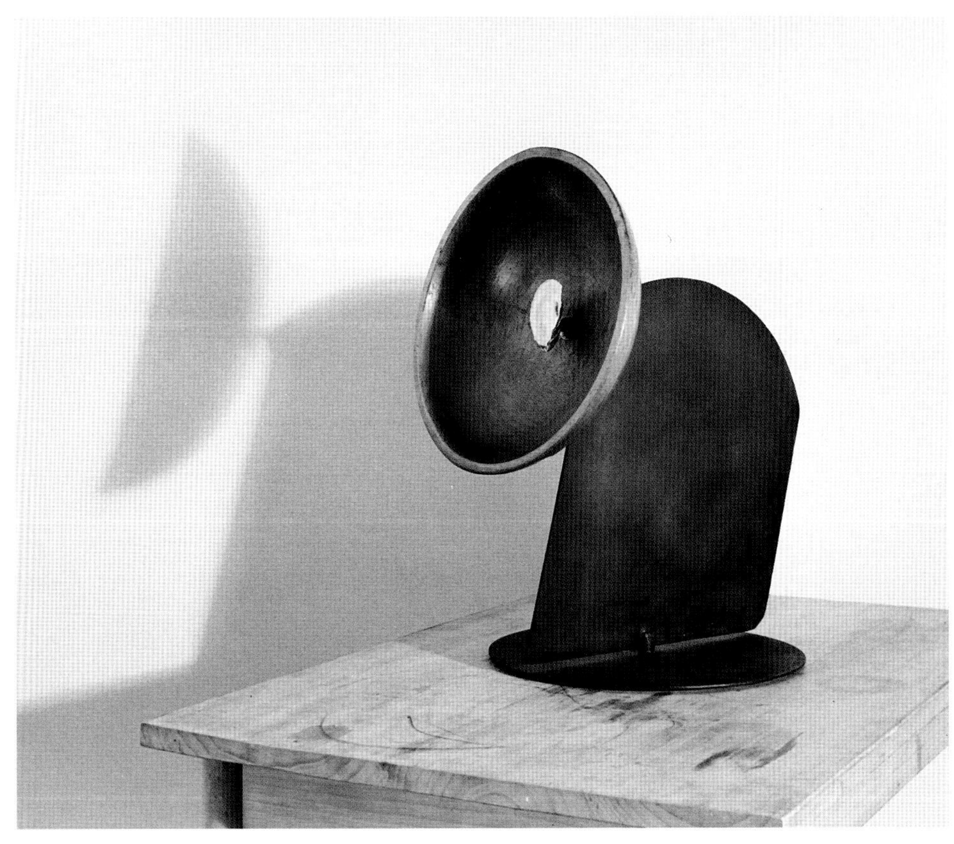

The Listener (San Francisco), 1997. Steel, wood, brass, and oyster shell. 24×15×15".

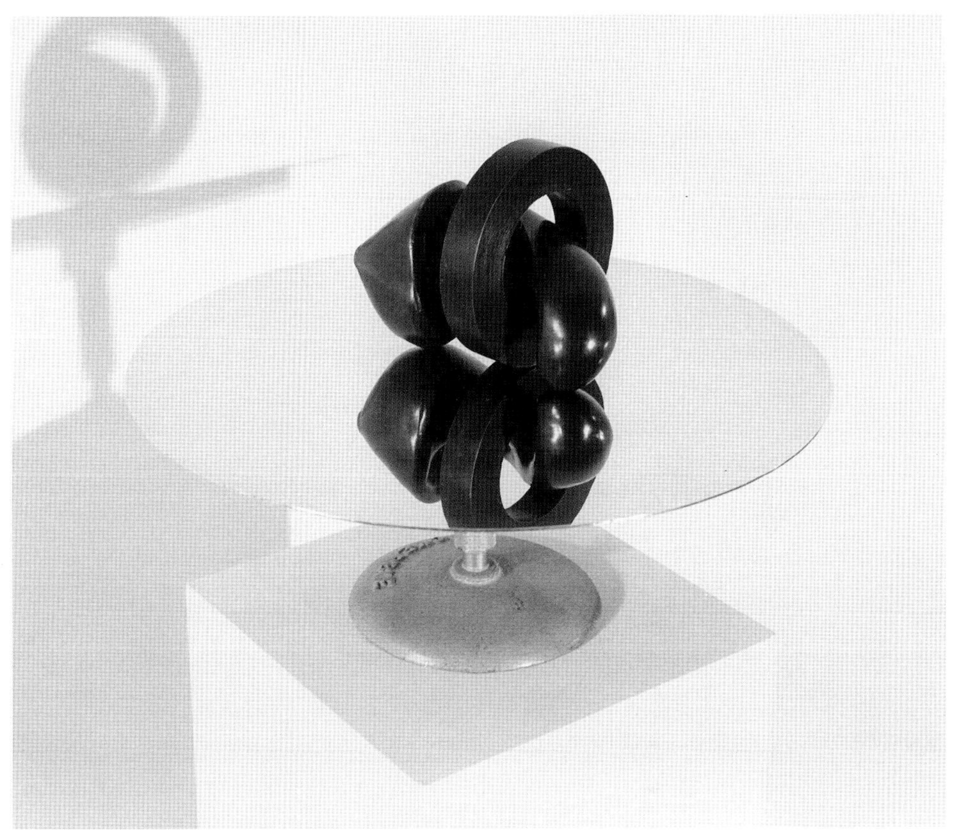

The Sleeper (Paris), 1997. Cast bronze on copper and aluminum base. 11×16×16".

TOM MARIONI

657 Howard Street, San Francisco, California 94105 • Phone/Fax: 415/495-3193

INDIVIDUAL EXHIBITIONS

1963   Bradley Memorial Museum of Art, Columbus GA [Sculpture]

1968   Richmond Art Center, Richmond CA [Sculpture]

1970   Oakland Art Museum, Oakland CA. " The Act of Drinking Beer with Friends is the Highest Form of Art" [Action and Installation]

1972   Richard Demarco Gallery, Edinburgh, Scotland [Sculpture]
DeSaisset Museum, University of Santa Clara CA [Installation]
Reese Palley Gallery, San Francisco CA - "A Seven Day Performance."

1975   Galeria Foksal, Warsaw, Poland - "Thinking Out Loud." [Installation]

1977   M H DeYoung Museum of Art, San Francisco CA - "The Sound of Flight."
Gallery Paule Anglim, San Francisco CA [Drawings]

1978   Los Angeles Institute of Contemporary Art, Los Angeles CA [Drawings]

1979   "The Museum of Conceptual Art at the San Francisco Museum of Modern Art",
San Francisco CA [Installation with Free Beer]
Modern Art Gallery, Vienna, Austria - [Installation]
Cochise Fine Arts Center, Bisbee AZ - "A Penny from Heaven." [Installation]

1980   Felix Handschin Gallery, Basel, Switzerland [Drawings]
Matrix, University Museum, University of California, Berkeley CA

1981   Site, Inc., San Francisco CA - "Paris, San Francisco, Kyoto [Installation]

1984   Gallery Paule Anglim, San Francisco CA [Drawings]
Le Consortium, Dijon, France - "Cutting the Mustard." [Installation]

1985   Eaton/Shoen Gallery, San Francisco, CA [Sculpture]

1986   New Langton Arts, San Francisco CA - "The Back Wall of MOCA."
Kuhlenschmidt/Simon, Los Angeles CA [Sculpture]

1987   Museo Italo Americano, San Francisco, CA - "The Italians, The Germans, The Japanese." [Sculpture]
Margarete Roeder Gallery, New York City NY [Sculpture]
Yoh Art Gallery, Osaka, Japan [Drawings]

1988   Artspace Annex, San Francisco CA - "Astronomy Piece." [Installation]
Margarete Roeder Gallery, New York City NY [Sculpture]

1989   Fuller Gross Gallery, San Francisco CA [Sculpture]

1990   Fuller Gross Gallery, San Francisco, CA [Sculpture]
Capp Street Project A.V.T., artist-in-residence, San Francisco CA - "The Artist's Studio (Starting Over)" [Installation]

1993   Gallery Paule Anglim, San Francisco CA - "Seascapes" [Sculpture]
Crown Point Press, San Francisco CA - "Landscapes" [Prints]
Robert Koch Gallery, San Francisco CA [Color Photograms]
University of Nevada, Reno NV [Installation]

1994   Margarete Roeder Gallery, New York City NY [Shadowgrams]

1995   Refusalon, San Francisco CA [Conceptual Works 1969-73]

1996   Gallery Paule Anglim, San Francisco CA [Sculpture]

1998   Gallery Paule Anglim, San Francisco CA [Sculpture]
        Margarete Roeder Gallery, New York, NY [Sculpture]

SELECTED GROUP EXHIBITIONS

1970   MOCA, San Francisco CA - "Sound Sculpture As." *

1971   DeSaisset Museum, University of Santa Clara CA - "Fish, Fox, Kos."

1972   Mills College Art Gallery, Oakland CA - "Notes and Scores for Sounds." *
        Newport Harbor Art Museum, Newport Beach CA - "The San Francisco
        Performance." *

1975   Biuro Wystaw Artyslycznych, Poland - "Kontra punkt."

1979   Salzburger Kunstverein, Austria - "Art as Photography."
        San Francisco Museum of Modern Art, San Francisco CA - "Space Time Sound."

1980   Academy der Kunst, Berlin, Germany - "For Eyes and Ears."
        ACR Museum of Modern Art, Paris, France - "For Eyes and Ears."
        Stedelijk Museum, Amsterdam, Netherlands - "Music/Sound/Language/Theater."

1982   Biennial II, San Francisco Museum of Modern Art, San Francisco CA - "Twenty
        Americans."
        Oakland Museum, CA - "100 Years of California Sculpture."
        Sound Art, Rimini Italy - "Sonorita Prospettiche."
        Los Angeles Institute of Contemporary Art, Los Angeles CA - "Sound."
        Belca House, Kyoto, Japan - "Elegant Miniatures from San Francisco." * [also at
        SF Museum of Modern Art, San Francisco CA]

1983   San Francisco Art Institute, CA - "Art Against War." *
        Franklin Furnace, New York NY - "In Other Words."

1984   The Sculpture Center, New York NY - "The Sound Art Show."
        San Antonio Art Museum, TX; Lock Haven Art Center, Orlando FL;
        Cranbrook Academy Museum, MI - "Awards in Visual Arts."

1985   Kunsthalle, Bern Switzerland - "Alles und Noch Viel Mehr." *
        Stuttgart Stratsgalerie, West Germany - "From Sound to Image."
        Oakland Museum, CA - "Art in the San Francisco Bay Area: 1945-1980."
        Otis Art Institute of the Parsons School of Design, Los Angeles, CA.
        "The Marriage of Art and Music for L.A." [installation for "New Music   America
        Festival.]

1986   San Francisco Art Institute, CA - "Inspired by Leonardo." *
        Gallery Route One, Pt. Reyes Station, CA. "Under One Roof."

1987   Banff Center, Alberta, Canada - "Object Lesson."

1988   Gallery Paule Anglim, San Francisco, CA - "Solid Concept."

1989   UCLA, San Jose CA, Fresno CA, Omaha NB museums - "Forty Years of California
        Assemblage."
        Hallwalls, Buffalo NY - "Bay Area Conceptualism: 2 Generations."

1990   University of Massachusetts, Amherst MA - "In Site."
        Sandra Gering Gallery, New York NY.

1992   Jernigan-Wicker Fine Art, San Francisco CA - John Cage Memorial

1993   LAMOCA, Guggenheim Soho NYC, Houston, Philadelphia, and Tokyo.
"Rolywholyover A Circus." (traveling show organized by John Cage).

1994   Gallery Paule Anglim, San Francisco - "Solid Concept 3."
Artists' Space, New York City NY - "Conceptual Art from the Bay Area." [Tom Marioni and David Ireland installations]
Crown Point Press, San Francisco CA [New Photogravures]

1995   INDEX Gallery, Osaka Japan. Benefit for the Kobe earthquake victims.
EXITART, New York City NY - "Endurance."
Museum of Contemporary Art, Los Angeles CA - "1965-1975 Reconsidering the Object of Art."

1996   Musees de Marseille, France - "The Art Embodied."

1998   Museum of Contemporary Art, Los Angeles CA - "Out of Actions: Between Performance and the Object 1949-1979."

* Organized

PERFORMANCE/ACTIONS

1966   Worked in night club, sketching nude model, San Francisco CA

1969   "One Second Sculpture," San Francisco CA
"Abstract Expressionistic Performance Sculpture," San Francisco CA

1970   "Sound Sculpture As," MOCA, San Francisco CA

1971   "Chain Reaction," DeSaisset Museum, University of Santa Clara CA
"Identity Transfer," Berkeley Gallery, San Francisco CA

1972   "Sunday Scottish Landscape," Richard Demarco Gallery, Edinburgh
"Sound Actions," Whitechapel Gallery, London England
"The Creation," Reese Palley Gallery, San Francisco

1973   "A Talk," Project, Inc., Boston, MA
MOCA Ensemble, St. Mary's Cathedral, Edinburgh Festival, Scotland
Concert, Institute of Contemporary Art, London, England
Concert, San Francisco Museum of Modern Art, San Francisco CA
Demonstration, University Art Museum, University of California, Berkeley
Radio performance, KPFA, Berkeley, CA

1974   "The Sun's Reception," residence of David and Mary Robinson, Sausalito CA
"A Sculpture in 2/3 Time," Student Cultural Center, Belgrade, Yugoslavia
"One Minute Demonstration," Gallery of Contemporary Art, Zagreb, Yugoslavia.
"Drum Lecture," 63 Bluxome Street, San Francisco CA

1975   "Duologue with Terry Fox," CARP, Los Angeles CA
"Morning Action," Salon of the Museum of Modern Art, Belgrade, Yugoslavia
"East/West," (with Petr Stembera), Prague, Czechoslovakia
"Thinking Out Loud," Galeria Foksal, Warsaw, Poland
"Lecture/reception/action," Indianapolis Museum of Art

1976   "Bird in Space: A Psychic Sculpture," And/Or Gallery, Seattle WA

1977   "Yellow is the Color of the Intellect," Portland Center for the Visual Arts,
"The Sound of Flight," M H DeYoung Museum of Art, San Francisco CA

1978   "Now We'll Have a Party," International Performance Biennial, Vienna
          Artist-in-residence, ZBS Media, New York State
          "Predictions," Alternative Art Space Conference, Los Angeles CA

1979   "Freibier (free beer)," Vienna Performance Biennial, Vienna Austria
          "A Social Action," Dany Keller Galerie, Munich, Germany
          "Action," Krinzinger Gallery, Innsbruck, Austria
          "Liberating Light and Sound," Pellegrino Gallery, Bologna, Italy
          "Talking Drumming," LACE, Los Angeles CA
          "A Theatrical Action to Define Non-theatrical Principles," Santa Barbara Museum
          of Art

1980   "Studio Bern," Kunst Museum, Bern, Switzerland
          "Studio Basel," Kunsthalle, Basel Switzerland
          "Bending Light," Berner Gallery, Bern, Switzerland
          "Atelier," Centre George Pompidou, Paris, France
          "Studio Berkeley," University Art Museum, University of California, Berkeley
          "Spirit in the Dark," Crown Point Press, Oakland CA
          "Studio Berlin," Akademie der Kunst, Berlin, West Germany
          "Word of Mouth," conference, Ponape Island, Pacific Ocean

1981   "Studio," tea house of the Saito Family, Kamakura, Japan
          "Studio Chicago," Museum of Contemporary Art, Chicago IL
          International Performance Festival, Lyon, France
          Performance Festival, Kunstlerhaus Bethanien, Berlin, West Germany

1982   University of California, San Diego CA
          Folkwang Museum, Essen, West Germany
          Kolnischer Kunstverein, Cologne, West Germany
          University of Wisconsin, Green Bay WI
          "Social Action," Intersection Theatre, Performance Festival, San Francisco CA
          "Studio Kyoto," Ohara Shrine, Kyoto, Japan (sponsored by Belca House)

1984   Consortium, Dijon, France

1985   Commencement speaker, Cincinnati Art Academy, Cincinnati OH

1986   "Double Portrait" with Shoichi Ida, The American Center, Kyoto, Japan

1996   WDR Radio, Cologne, Germany. Performance. Acoustic Festival

1997   The Art Orchestra, California Palace of the Legion of Honor, San Francisco

RELATED PROFESSIONAL ACTIVITIES

1968-1971   Curator of Art, Richmond Art Center, Richmond CA

1970-1984   Founding Director, Museum of Conceptual Art (MOCA), San Francisco CA

1973-1974   Founding Director, MOCA Ensemble, a free jazz group

1975-1982   Editor/Designer, *Vision,* art journal published by Crown Point Press, Oakland

1981   Artist-in-Residence, Djerassi Foundation, Woodside CA

1990   Artist-in-Residence, Pilchuck Glass School, Stanwood WA
               Artist-in-Residence, The Fabric Workshop, Philadelphia PA

1992   Consultant for public art, Central Embarcadero project, City of San Francisco

1997   Founder and Composer, The Art Orchestra, a sculptors ensemble

AWARDS, GRANTS AND FELLOWSHIPS

1976   National Endowment for the Arts: Sculpture

1980   National Endowment for the Arts: Sculpture

1981   John Simon Guggenheim Memorial: Conceptual Art

1984   National Endowment for the Arts: Sculpture
          Awards in the Visual Arts: Sculpture

1986   Asian Cultural Council: Travel Grant/Japan

COMMISSIONS

1988   Public sculpture, Marin County Civic Center, San Rafael CA "Observatory Bird."

1990   "The Yellow Sound for Kandinsky," West Deutscher Rundfunk (German radio),
          Cologne, Germany.

BIBLIOGRAPHY

Cover story. *Pacific Sun,* 7-13 July 1971, San Rafael CA.

"Man of Sound Vision." *The Guardian,* 5 June 1972, Glasgow, Scotland.

Interview. *Studio International,* June 1972.

"Activity as Sculpture," (interview *Art and Artists,* August 1973, London.

"Kalifornia 'artionismus'." *der Lowe #1,* 1974, Bern, Switzerland.

Il Corpo Come Lingvaggio (La Body Art). 1974, Milan, Italy.

The Painted Word. Tom Wolfe. 1975, p. 107-08.

"Deja Vu." *San Francisco Magazine,* December 1976, p. 94-95.

"Mellow Marioni still off the Wall." Thomas Albright, *San Francisco Chronicle,* 30 April 1977.

Report from San Francisco. Carter Ratcliff, *Art in America,* May/June 1977.

"Tom Marioni and the Sound of Flight." Bill Kleb, *Artweek,* 4 June 1977, p.7.

"An Artist's Right to Remain Silent." Thomas Albright, *San Francisco Chronicle,* 29 Sept. 1977.

"Toward a History of California Performance: Part One." Moira Roth, *Arts,* February 1978.

"Denk-Bilder." von Walter Beyer, *Observer,* 13 June 1979, Vienna Austria.

Review. (Galerie Dany Keller) *Suddentsce Zeitung,* 23 June 1979.

Performance Anthology-California Performance Art. 1980, Contemporary Arts Press, San
     Francisco.

Review. Alan G. Artner, *The Chicago Tribune,* Jan 23, 1981.

Review. Kunstmuseum Bern performance. *Der Bund,* Bern Switzerland, 6 June 1980.

Frank Cebulski, *Artweek,* 14 Aug 1982.

Marioni a Master Illusionist's Act." Thomas Albright, *San Francisco Chronicle,* 17 August 1982.

"The Merging of Visual Arts with the Theater." Thomas Albright, *S.F. Chronicle,* 22 August 1982.

"Establishing an Object's Worth." (review) Christopher French, *Artweek,* 28 Jan 1984.

Art in the San Francisco Bay Area. 1945-1980. Thomas Albright, University of California Press, 1985.

"Interview #32." Barbara Smith, *High Performance,* November 1985.

Review. Kenneth Baker, *San Francisco Chronicle,* 4 January 1986.

Review. Charles Shere, *The Tribune,* 14 January 1986. Oakland CA.

Review. Will Torphy, *Artweek,* 25 January 1986. San Francisco CA.

Interview. Jamie Brunson, *Expo-see,* Spring 1986, #19, San Francisco CA.

Review. Bill Berkson, *Artforum,* May 1986.

Review. David Winter, *Artnews,* April 1986.

Review. Kristine McKenna, *Los Angeles Times,* 8 August 1986.

Review. Mark Levy, *Art in America,* June 1987.

Review. Charles Shere, *The Tribune,* 19 February 1987, Oakland CA.

Review. Kenneth Baker, *S.F. Chronicle,* 18 February 1987.

Review. Leslie Dawn, *Vanguard,* 12/87-1/88.

Review. Robert Atkins, *Village Voice,* October 1988.

Review. Ken Johnson, *Art in America,* February 1989.

Review. Mark Levy, Art International, Spring 1989, p. 66.

"Shadow Boxes Hold Wit, Art Homages." Kenneth Baker, *San Francisco Chronicle,* 17 Feb. 1990.

"Significant Engagement." (review) Terri Cohn, *Artweek,* 7 June 1990.

"Art Through the Eye of a Beer Glass." (review) David Bonetti, *San Francisco Examiner,* 8 June 1990.

Review. Kenneth Baker, *San Francisco Chronicle,* 16 June 1990.

Review. Kenneth Baker, *San Francisco Chronicle,* 14 February 1993.

"Playing with Chance and Process." David Bonetti, *San Francisco Examiner,* 17 February 1993.

Review. Marcia Tanner, *Artnews,* April 1993.

Review. Kenneth Baker, *San Francisco Chronicle,* Sept. 17, 1993.

PUBLIC COLLECTIONS

Oakland Museum

Santa Barbara Museum of Art

Newport Harbor Art Museum, Newport Beach CA

San Francisco Museum of Modern Art

Regional Collections, Dijon France

Museum of Modern Art, New York City NY

Stadtische Kunsthalle, Mannheim Germany

Chase Manhattan Bank, New York City NY

M.H. DeYoung Memorial Museum, San Francisco

Photographs: Robert Adrian 25. Kathan Brown 26. Ben Blackwell 23. Lee Fatheree 38, 44, 45, 46, 47, 48, 49, 50. Larry Fox 17, 18, 19. Marion Gray 15, 64, 65. Dan Herth 4, 8. Paul Hoffman 43, 56, 57.